MICKEY ROGERS
JOANNE TAYLORE-KNOWLES
STEVE TAYLORE-KNOWLES

SPEAK YOUR MIND

STUDENT'S BOOK
+ access to Student's App and Digital Workbook

1

macmillan education

	Outcomes	Vocabulary	Grammar	Speaking
Unit 1 Who Are You? pp. 7–15	• Describe who you are and what you like in an online profile • Greet and introduce people in various settings • Complete registration information with numbers	• Forms • Greetings, introductions, and goodbyes • Ordinal numbers	• *Be* statements and *yes/no* questions • Information questions with *be* Grammar Reference pp. 142–143	• Describe people • Make introductions • Give personal information
	Language and Life—Communication: Make an Interesting Online Profile			
Unit 2 Work/Life Balance pp. 17–25	• Talk about various jobs • Talk about members of your family • Discuss your family members and their jobs	• Work life • Family • Jobs	• Articles *a*, *an*, and no article • Possessive adjectives and *'s/s'* Grammar Reference pp. 143–144	• Talk about a famous person • Talk about family • Describe a picture
	Language and Life—Self-awareness: Find the Right Job for Your Interests and Abilities			
Unit 3 Fun and Games pp. 27–35	• Express likes and dislikes • Talk about and recommend free-time activities • Plan and talk about an event	• Likes and dislikes • Free-time activities • Special events	• Simple present statements and *yes/no* questions • The imperative Grammar Reference pp. 145–146	• Talk about things you like to do • Recommend free-time activities • Describe an event
	Language and Life—Creativity: Create an Interest Group for a Website			
Unit 4 That's Life! pp. 37–45	• Talk about daily activities • Talk about how often you do activities • Describe your day off	• Daily activities • Frequency and time expressions • Routine activities	• Simple present information questions • Frequency adverbs Grammar Reference pp. 146–147	• Interview a partner about daily activities • Talk about routine activities • Discuss the perfect day off
	Language and Life—Adaptability: Give Advice about Keeping Life Interesting			
Unit 5 Finding Your Way pp. 47–55	• Talk about places to live • Describe your neighborhood • Give directions	• Where you live • Places in a neighborhood • Directions	• Adjectives • *There is / There are* Grammar Reference pp. 148–149	• Talk about where you live • Discuss a neighborhood • Give directions
	Language and Life—Problem-solving: Create a Guide to Your Neighborhood			
Unit 6 Going Viral pp. 57–65	• Talk about social media use • Talk about computer equipment and vlogging • Talk about buying and selling online	• Emotions • Technology equipment • Technology phrases	• Present progressive • Present progressive vs. simple present Grammar Reference pp. 149–150	• Talk about routines and feelings • Discuss vlogs • Discuss online activity
	Language and Life—Critical Thinking: Analyze the Pros and Cons of A Digital Detox			

Confident Communicator	Pronunciation	Listening/Reading	Thinking Skills	Writing
Repair It • Ask for repetition *Start Talking* • Add details *Start Talking* • Useful phrases	• Intonation in *yes/no* and information questions	Read a social media profile • Skill—Infer information Listen to short conversations of greetings • Skill—Listen for details Listen for personal details • Skill—Listen for numerical information	• Evaluate • Deduce	Write about a school calendar
Unit Review p. 16	**Study Skills** p. 127—Memory Strategies			
Keep Talking • Useful phrases *Repair It* • Check for understanding *Keep Talking* • Use notes	• *An* + vowel	Read an online article about a business owner • Skill—Scan Listen to a conversation about a family picture • Skill—Use visual clues Listen to a description of a family vacation picture • Skill—Predict	• Question • Analyze • Categorize	Write an online family profile
Unit Review p. 26	**Follow A Pro** p. 128—An IT Consultant ▶ An IT Professional			
Keep Talking • Emphasize preference *Keep Talking* • Give reasons *Keep Talking* • Express rules	• Third person *–s*	Read a magazine interview • Skill—Infer Listen to a phone conversation about an event • Skill—Take notes Listen to a recorded advertisement • Skill—Listen for gist	• Categorize • Understand • Recall	Create a poster to advertise a special event
Unit Review p. 36	**Study Skills** p. 129—Oral Presentations			
Start Talking • Give examples *Keep Talking* • Useful phrases *Keep Talking* • Express frequency	• Word stress in information questions	Read a blog post about a reporter's day • Skill—Scan Listen to an interview with an actress • Skill—Listen for specific information Listen to a radio show about daily routines • Skill—Listen for gist	• Analyze • Summarize • Recall	Write about the perfect day off
Unit Review p. 46	**Follow A Pro** p. 130—A Firefighter ▶ A Paramedic			
Keep Talking • Make guesses *Keep Talking* • Useful phrases *Start Talking* • Useful phrases	• Syllable stress in multi-syllable adjectives	Read an article about unusual places to live • Skill—Scan for specific information Listen to a radio show about neighborhoods • Skill—Listen for specific information Listen to conversations asking for directions • Skill—Listen for key words	• Apply • Evaluate • Analyze	Write an instant message
Unit Review p. 56	**Study Skills** p. 131—Research Skills			
Start Talking • Useful phrases *Keep Talking* • Show interest *Keep Talking* • Ask follow-up questions	• /ŋ/	Read an article about social media use and employment • Skill—Predict information Listen to vloggers describe their videos • Skill—Listen for fact and opinion Listen to an internet business owner • Skill—Listen for the main idea	• Analyze • Evaluate	Write a social media ad
Unit Review p. 66	**Follow A Pro** p. 132—A Chief Listening Officer ▶ A Social Media Manager			

	Outcomes	Vocabulary	Grammar	Speaking
Unit 7 Fit for Life pp. 67–75	• Talk about parts of the body and abilities • Talk about sports and athletes • Describe skills and abilities	• Parts of the body • Ball game action words • Exercise words	• *Can/can't* (ability) • Adverbs of manner Grammar Reference pp. 151–152	• Talk about abilities • Describe a famous athlete • Role-play a job interview
	Language and Life—Decision-making: Design an Outdoor Gym for Your City			
Unit 8 Foodie? pp. 77–85	• Talk about food and tastes • Talk about types of food and ingredients • Follow and write a recipe	• Food and tastes • Food groups • Cooking	• Countable and uncountable nouns • *This/that/these/those* Grammar Reference pp. 152–153	• Talk about food preference • Discuss and recommend healthy foods • Discuss recipes
	Language and Life—Communication: Design a Restaurant Guide			
Unit 9 Seeing the World pp. 87–95	• Talk about travel • Give advice and suggestions • Talk about clothes to wear on a trip	• Travel • Tourism collocations • Clothes	• Verb + infinitive or gerund • *Should/could* for advice and possibility Grammar Reference pp. 154–155	• Plan a virtual tour • Role-play a phone conversation • Discuss a planned trip
	Language and Life—Collaboration: Create an Advertisement to Attract Tourists			
Unit 10 Life Stories pp. 97–105	• Talk about life events • Talk about your social life • Describe a personal experience	• From the reading • Social life collocations • Collocations with *get, have,* and *make*	• Simple past (affirmative statements) • Simple past (negative statements and questions) Grammar Reference pp. 155–156	• Talk about milestones • Discuss events in the past • Talk about a specific experience from the past
	Language and Life—Empathy: Give Advice Based on Your Experience for an Advice Column			
Unit 11 Planning Ahead pp. 107–115	• Talk about plans and intentions • Give and receive advice for saving money • Talk about career goals	• To-do lists • Money • Career plans collocations	• *Going to* • Direct and indirect objects Grammar Reference pp. 157–158	• Talk about predictions and plans • Role-play a conversation about saving money • Discuss career plans
	Language and Life—Self-direction: Make a Career Plan Based On Your Interests			
Unit 12 The Great Outdoors pp. 117–125	• Discuss climate and weather • Talk about natural features in geography • Describe outdoor activities	• From the reading • Natural features • Adjectives to describe natural features	• Comparative adjectives • Review of tenses Grammar Reference pp. 158–159	• Discuss weather • Talk about a natural place • Talk about outdoor activities
	Language and Life—Problem-solving: Present Ideas for Developing a Natural Area			

Confident Communicator	Pronunciation	Listening/Reading	Thinking Skills	Writing
Start Talking • Useful phrases *Start Talking* • Buy time *Keep Talking* • Use imagination	• *Can/can't*	Read a magazine article about fitness gadgets • Skill—Read for gist Listen to people describe unusual sports • Skill—Listen for the main idea Listen to descriptions of exercises • Skill—Listen for specific information	• Analyze • Deduce • Evaluate	Write an email inquiring about a job
Unit Review p. 76 **Study Skills** p. 133—Effective Group Work				
Start Talking • Useful phrases *Keep Talking* • Useful phrases *Repair It* • Check for understanding	• Emphasis with *this/that/these/ those*	Read posts from an online food forum • Skill—Read for the main idea Listen to an interview with street food vendors • Skill—Listen for specific information Listen to the steps of a recipe • Skill—Listen for specific information	• Apply • Analyze • Evaluate	Write a recipe
Unit Review p. 86 **Follow A Pro** p. 134—A Food Stylist ▶ A Baker				
Keep Talking • Take time to think *Keep Talking* • Useful phrases *Start Talking* • Follow-up questions	• *to*	Read an article about virtual travel • Skill—Scan Listen to a radio show about tourism • Skill—Listen for detail Listen to people talk about packing for a trip • Skill—Listen for gist	• Analyze • Recall • Deduce	Write advice for tourists
Unit Review p. 96 **Study Skills** p. 135—Formal vs. Informal Writing				
Start Talking • Useful phrases *Keep Talking* • Show interest *Start Talking* • Useful phrases	• the ending *–ed*	Read a biography on Malala Yousafzai • Skill—Scan for information Listen to a conversation about social life • Skill—Listen for main ideas Listen to personal stories • Skill—Listen for gist	• Summarize • Evaluate • Analyze	Write an email about a personal experience
Unit Review p. 106 **Follow A Pro** p. 136—An Event Organizer ▶ A Tour Guide				
Start Talking • Useful phrases *Keep Talking* • Suggest alternatives *Repair It* • Useful phrases	• *Going to*	Read an article about to-do lists • Skill—Read for the main idea Listen to a radio show about money • Skill—Listen for specific information Listen to a podcast about dream jobs • Skill—Listen for gist	• Apply • Calculate • Analyze	Write a journal entry about career plans
Unit Review p. 116 **Study Skills** p. 137—Personal Development				
Keep Talking • Useful phrases *Keep Talking* • Show interest *Keep Talking* • Useful phrases	• /ju/	Read a brochure about the Galapagos Islands • Skill—Scan for specific information Listen to a radio interview about waterfalls • Skill—Listen for specific information Listen to a conversation about visiting natural places in Mexico • Skill—Listen for detail	• Understand • Induce • Recall	Write a guidebook entry about a natural feature
Unit Review p. 126 **Follow A Pro** p. 138—A Forest Ranger ▶ A Botanist				

Grammar Quiz: What Do You Already Know?

A Choose the correct option.

1 I'm am not / I'm not / I isn't Brazilian.
2 Am / Is / Are your teacher from Peru?
3 It's / It / It not nice to meet you.
4 Where be / is / are they from?
5 What is / are / does your last name?
6 We am / is / are not Spanish students.

B Complete the paragraph with the simple present form of the verbs in parentheses.

Many students **1** ______________ (not know) what they want to do after they finish college. But I do. I **2** ______________ (want) to be a flight attendant. Flight attendants **3** ______________ (travel) the world, and I **4** ______________ (love) to travel! My friend Beth **5** ______________ (work) as a flight attendant now. She **6** ______________ (not make) a lot of money, but she's happy.

C Complete the sentences with the present progressive form of the verbs in the box.

cook not do not listen rain wear work

1 It ______________ outside. Don't forget to take your umbrella.
2 The teacher is angry because the students ______________.
3 Harry has a great job. He ______________ at the office in Spain right now.
4 Sorry, I can't talk right now. I ______________ dinner.
5 Calvin ______________ the laundry now because he doesn't have any soap.
6 Dan ______________ shorts and a T-shirt because it's very hot today.

D Unscramble and write sentences.

1 listen / we / to / sometimes / music / .
____
2 I / where / vegetables / buy / can / ?
____
3 never / is / our / teacher / late / .
____
4 hair / long / Sally / has / brown / .
____
5 there / many / eggs / how / are / ?
____
6 cook / does / Adam / how / often / ?
____

E Find one error in each sentence. Write the correct sentence.

1 My fathers' name is Antonio.
____
2 Please take a umbrella with you.
____
3 Why do you have three cell phone?
____
4 Don't to forget to come to my party.
____
5 Jeff take the train to work.
____
6 We have any tomatoes.
____

Go to the Grammar Review on pages 140–141.

UNIT 1

Who Are You?

WHAT DO YOU ALREADY KNOW?

1 **Think of words you know that describe you. Write the words.**

2 **IN PAIRS** **Share and compare your words. If possible, add more words to the box.**

I am ...

VIDEO

DISCUSS & SHARE

3 **IN GROUPS** **Watch the video and answer the question.**

SYM Are you typical or different?

In this unit, you will ...

- describe yourself, introduce yourself and others, and give personal details about yourself.
- use thinking skills: evaluate and draw conclusions.
- read about a social media profile.
- use strategies to start talking and keep talking by asking for repetition or asking for details.
- use communication skills to create an interesting social media profile.
- learn strategies for memorization.

LESSON 1 About You

READING

A Are you on any social media sites? Which ones? Discuss.

B 1.01 READING SKILL—Infer information **Read the form. Then choose the correct answer.**

International English Teachers

ABOUT YOU

I'm an English teacher in Germany. I'm from Berlin. I speak German, English, and Spanish. My hobbies are swimming, dancing, and yoga. My favorite music is rock and my favorite food is tacos (♥ Mexican food). My boyfriend is Juan. He isn't an English teacher. He's a yoga teacher.

Username:	Berliner100	Last name:	Steiner
Password:	DerSeestern!	Nickname:	Angie
Re-enter password:	DerSeestern!	Date of birth:	04/15/97
First name:	Angela	Country:	Germany

Your Profile

Edit Profile

1 Is this an English-language website? Yes, it is. / No, it isn't.
2 Is Angie Steiner the name on her passport? Yes, it is. / No, it isn't.
3 Is the number 04 a month? Yes, it is. / No, it isn't.
4 Is she from Europe? Yes, she is. / No, she isn't.
5 Is she a yoga teacher? Yes, she is. / No, she isn't.
6 Is she married? Yes, she is. / No, she isn't.

C THINKING SKILL—Evaluate **Consider why some passwords are secure and others are not secure.**

VOCABULARY

A **Match the personal information (1–6) to a category (a–f). Write the letter.**

1 11/18/90 ____ a last name
2 Robert ____ b nickname
3 US ____ c hobby
4 Garcia ____ d date of birth
5 playing video games ____ e first name
6 Robbie ____ f country

B **Complete the profile for you. Then share with a partner.**

First name ____________ Date of birth ____________
Last name ____________ Country ____________
Nickname ____________ Hobbies ____________

A: My first name is Amanda. And you? *B: My first name is Olivia. My last name is …*

GRAMMAR *be* statements and *yes/no* questions

A IN PAIRS **Complete the examples.**

Affirmative	Negative
1 I ______ / I'm an English teacher. 2 We are / We'______ English students. 3 He ______ / He's a yoga teacher.	4 I am not / I'm ______ from Mexico. 5 They are not / They're not / They ______ German teachers. 6 He is not / He's not / He ______ an English teacher.

Questions and Short Answers

7 Are you late? Yes, I am. / No, I'm ______.
8 Is she married? Yes, she ______. / No, she's not. / No, she isn't.
9 Are they from Berlin? Yes, they are. / No, ______ not. / No, they aren't.

For more practice, go to page 142.

B **Complete with the correct forms of *be*.**

1 ______ you a student? No, I ______. I ______ a teacher.
2 ______ your parents from Mexico? No, they ______. They ______ from Brazil.
3 ______ your English teacher American? Yes, he ______.
4 ______ I in the correct classroom? No, you ______. This ______ English 5.

C **Complete the answers for you.**

1 Are you on social media?
Yes, I'm on two social media sites.
2 Is your favorite hobby playing video games?
______
3 Is your favorite food from your country?
______
4 Are your parents from this city?
______

MAKE IT REAL

Informal ways to say Yes: *Yeah, Uh-huh, Yep*
Informal ways to say No: *Uh-uh, Nope, No way*

D IN PAIRS **Ask and answer the questions in C.**

SPEAKING

A **Complete the survey for you.**

About me ...

From	Nickname	Favorite food
Hobbies	Birth month	Favorite music

B IN GROUPS **Ask questions and try to guess your partner's answers. Use the Confident Communicator box to help you.**

A: Are you from Brazil? *B: No, I'm not.*
C: Are you from Mexico? *B: Yes, I am.*

CONFIDENT COMMUNICATOR
REPAIR IT

When you don't understand or don't hear something, ask for repetition.
Excuse me?
Sorry, can you repeat that, please?

LESSON 2 Hello and Goodbye

LISTENING

A Look at the pictures (a–c). Match the pictures to the questions (1–4).

a

b

c

1 How do you greet a good friend or a family member? _____
2 How do you greet a new classmate? _____
3 How do you greet an important person for the first time? _____
4 How do you greet someone you don't know well? _____

B 1.02 THINKING SKILL—Deduce Listen. Check (✓) if the people know each other.

1 ☐ Sandy and Jake
2 ☐ Janice Walters and Lynn Jefferson
3 ☐ Mr. Wilson and Sarah
4 ☐ Christine, Mark, and Jean Luc

C 1.02 LISTENING SKILL—Listen for details Listen again and choose the correct answer.

1 Where is Michelle?
a at work
b at home
c with Jake

2 Who is the office manager?
a Lynn
b Ms. Jefferson
c Janice

3 Why is Mr. Wilson at DT Bank?
a to work
b to talk about his account
c to get money

4 What country is Jean Luc from?
a France
b the US
c Canada

VOCABULARY greetings, introductions, and goodbyes

A Complete the table with phrases from the box.

Bye.	Good morning.	Hey!
~~Hi.~~	How's it going?	~~I'm John Smith.~~
Nice to meet you.	See you later.	How are you?
~~Take care.~~	This is Nicolle Martin.	It's nice to meet you.

MAKE IT YOURS

Can you think of situations when you have to introduce someone in English?

Greetings	Introductions	Goodbyes
Hi.	*I'm John Smith.*	*Take care.*

B **Complete the conversation with words and phrases from A.**

Kara: 1 ____________, Josie. How's 2 ____________?

Josie: 3 ____________, Kara. I'm good. 4 ____________?

Kara: Fine, thanks. Josie, 5 ____________ my friend Michelle Kim.

Josie: Hi, Michelle. I'm Josie Grayson. It's 6 ____________.

Michelle: 7 ____________, too, Josie.

Kara: Well, it's good to see you, Josie. 8 ____________.

Josie: Nice to see you, too. 9 ____________.

MAKE IT REAL

In informal situations, people use very short and informal forms of greetings and goodbyes.

Greetings:	Goodbyes:
What's up?	*Later!*
How you doing?	*Catch you later.*
What's new?	*See ya!*

C **IN GROUPS** **Practice the conversation in B using your own names.**

GRAMMAR information questions with *be*

A **Complete the table with *what, where, when,* or *how*.**

Question Word + *be* + Word or Phrase	Answer
Who is your teacher?	Mr. Oliver is my teacher.
1 ________ is your name?	My name is Lisette.
2 ________ is Mandy?	She's at the office in Chicago.
3 ________ is your birthday?	It's in May.
4 ________ are you?	I'm fine, thanks.

For more practice, go to page 142.

B **Complete the questions and answers for you.**

1 ____________'s your name? It's ____________.
2 ____________ old are you? I'm ____________.
3 ____________ are you from? I'm from ____________.
4 ____________ is your birthday? It's in ____________. (month)
5 ____________ is your favorite singer? My favorite singer is ____________.

C **IN PAIRS** **Ask and answer the questions in B.**

SPEAKING

A **IN GROUPS** **Greet classmates you know. Introduce yourself to classmates you do not know. Ask questions to find out more information about each person.**

A: Hi. I'm Sal. How's it going?
B: Great. I'm Leslie. How are you, Sal?
A: Fine, thanks. Where are you from?
B: I'm from Port-au-Prince, Haiti. Where are you from?

B **Introduce someone to your class. The person you introduce then introduces someone else. Use the Confident Communicator box to help you.**

CONFIDENT COMMUNICATOR
START TALKING

When we introduce someone, it is common to give a little more information about the person.
This is Robert. He's my neighbor. He's from Chicago.

VOCABULARY ordinal numbers

A 1.03 **Write the ordinal numbers for the days of the month.**

APRIL						
SUNDAY	MONDAY	TUESDAY	WEDNESDAY	THURSDAY	FRIDAY	SATURDAY
	1 first	2 second	3 third	4 fourth	5 fifth	6 sixth
7 seventh	8 eighth	9 ninth	10 tenth	11 eleventh	12 twelfth	13 thirteenth
14 fourteenth	15 fifteenth	16 **1** ________	17 seventeenth	18 eighteenth	19 nineteenth	20 twentieth
21 **2** ________	22 **3** ________	23 twenty-third	24 twenty-fourth	25 twenty-fifth	26 twenty-sixth	27 **4** ________
28 **5** ________	29 twenty-ninth	30 thirtieth				

B IN PAIRS **Complete the sentences for you. Then discuss.**

1 My birthday is ____________.

2 Today is ____________.

3 New Year's Day is ____________.

4 My favorite holiday is ____________, on ____________.

5 In my family, I am the ____________ child.

LISTENING

A IN PAIRS THINKING SKILL—Evaluate **Make a list of dates that are important to you. Ask your partner why his/her dates are important.**

A: Why is August 2 important to you? Is it your birthday? *B: Yes, it is.*

B 1.04 LISTENING SKILL—Listen for numerical information **Listen to the conversation and answer the questions.**

MAKE IT REAL

Write dates with cardinal numbers: April 4.
Say dates with ordinal numbers: April fourth (4th).
US: write dates as month, day, year: 10/22/2019.
UK: write dates as day, month, year: 22/10/19.

1 What is Olivia's date of birth? ____________
2 What is her address? ____________
3 Is her phone number 555-376-5832? ____________
4 How much money is the registration? ____________
5 When does Olivia's group start? ____________
6 Is this her first marathon? ____________

PRONUNCIATION intonation in *yes/no* and information questions

A 1.04 **Listen again. Draw an arrow pointing up if the speaker's voice goes up at the end of the question. Draw an arrow pointing down if the speaker's voice goes down at the end of the question.**

What is your first name? ↘

Is registration open? ↗

1 What's your last name?

2 And your phone number?

3 What is your date of birth?

4 Is this your first marathon?

B IN PAIRS **Ask and answer the questions from A. Use correct intonation for *yes/no* and information questions.**

WRITING

A Read the rules for capital letters. Then correct the capitalization mistakes in the text.

Capitalize:

- names of people, pets, places: Daniel, San Francisco, my cat Coco
- countries, nationalities, languages: Ecuador, British, Chinese
- months, days, holidays: January, Monday, Independence Day
- the pronoun *I*
- the first letter of the first word in a sentence

Adams English Academy Academic Calendar

August 21–September 2	registration opens
September 2	fall semester begins
December 10	fall semester ends
December 15–January 5	school closed
January 6–10	registration opens
January 11	spring semester begins

i am a student at Adams english Academy. Registration is from August 21st to September 2nd. The first day of class is on September 2nd. The first semester is from September 2nd to December 10th. The school is closed from December 15th to January 5th for the new Year holiday. the next semester is from january 11th to May 3rd. I'm in the first level, and my teacher is Robert green. His nickname is rob.

B Write about your English class or school. Use the paragraph in A as a model. Remember to use capital letters.

SPEAKING

A IN PAIRS **Read the questions out loud and answer them as quickly as you can. Use the Confident Communicator box to help you.**

1 What is the eighth month of the year? ______

2 What is the fourteenth letter of the English alphabet? ______

3 What is the day after the last day of the year? ______

4 What is two days after the second day of the weekend? ______

5 What is the extra day in February? ______

6 What is the 365th day of the year? ______

7 Write your own: ______

B IN GROUPS **Check your answers. How many pairs got 100% correct?**

CONFIDENT COMMUNICATOR

START TALKING

To talk about numbers in math, say:

\+ *plus* – *minus* × *times* ÷ *divided by* = *equals*

Five plus two equals seven, and five minus three equals two.

Language and Life

Communication – Online Profiles

A 1.05 **Read the online article. Choose *True* or *False*.**

SOCIAL MEDIA PROFILE TIPS

Many social media websites have different parts in the personal profile section.

One part is often about specific preferences—movies, books, TV shows, and sports. Another part is for biographical information. When you create a social media profile, here are some things to consider:

- Are your preferences interesting?
- Is your personal information interesting? Write one or two interesting things about yourself!
- Is your information safe? Don't write your home address, phone number, or vacation dates.
- Are your grammar and spelling correct? Your language is part of your reputation!
- Finally, is your picture good? Use a clear picture of yourself.

1 This is a social media website. True / False
2 Many social media profiles have different sections. True / False
3 Your entertainment preferences are a part of your personality. True / False
4 It's a good idea to include your phone number and address in your profile. True / False
5 Grammar and spelling are not important in a social media profile. True / False

B IN PAIRS **Help Amanda improve her profile. Circle and correct five capitalization errors and one grammar error.**

SYM INSTITUTE

HOME | CALENDAR | FACULTY | STAFF | ORGANIZATION | STUDENT PROFILES

Basics
Name: Amanda herrero
Age: 20
Hometown: Recife
English level or class: 1B (Beginner)

Interests/Favorites
Music/Musicians: pop—Ed Sheeran, Camila Cabello; reggaeton
Games: *League of Legends*
People I like: Beyoncé, Bill and Melinda Gates, Neymar
Hobbies: dancing, going out to eat, beach parties
Other: my cats, my boyfriend julio

More About Me
I'm a student in communications at the Federal university of Pernambuco, in recife. My favorite Things is my pets and my car (an old Volkswagen Beetle!).

C **Circle two things for Amanda to add to the Basics section and three things for her to add to the Interests/Favorites section.**

Basics

Address	Email address
Birthday	Hair and eye color
Brothers and sisters	Phone number
Country	Social media sites

Interests/Favorites

Actors	Movies
Animals	Places
Apps	Sports
Clothes	TV shows
Food/restaurants	

D **Write questions Amanda can use as ideas for the More About Me section.**

Who's your favorite person in the world?
What is your favorite animal?

1 ______________________________
2 ______________________________
3 ______________________________
4 ______________________________
5 ______________________________

E **Complete a profile for you.**

HOME | CALENDAR | FACULTY | STAFF | ORGANIZATION | STUDENT PROFILES

Upload Photo

Basics

Name: ______________________________
Age: ______________________________
Hometown: ______________________________
English level or class: ______________________________

Interests/Favorites

Music/Musicians: ______________________________
Games: ______________________________
People: ______________________________
Social activities: ______________________________
Other: ______________________________

More About Me

____
____
____
____
____

F **IN PAIRS Read your partner's profile. Make suggestions to improve the profile. Does your partner ...**

capitalize words correctly?	Yes / No
use *be* correctly?	Yes / No
describe herself/himself?	Yes / No

MAKE IT DIGITAL

Join an English-language social media site. Use some of the ideas in this lesson to create your profile.

VOCABULARY review

SCORE: / 10

A Complete the paragraph with words from the box.

favorite first food hello hobbies hometown meet nice nickname up

1 ________! What's **2** ________? My name is Manuel. My **3** ________ is Manny. I'm from El Salvador. My **4** ________ is Santa Ana. I'm 16 and a student. My **5** ________ are swimming and playing soccer. My **6** ________ music is pop and my favorite **7** ________ is pizza. My birthday is August **8** ________. It's **9** ________ to **10** ________ you!

GRAMMAR review

SCORE: / 10

A Unscramble the sentences. Use the correct form of *be*.

1. from Brazil / my parents / be / . ________
2. I / on social media / not / be / . ________
3. teachers / they / be / ? ________
4. last name / your / Stevens / be / ? ________
5. I / your English class / in / be / ? ________

B Complete the questions.

1. ________ your name? My name's Celia.
2. ________ it going? Great, thanks.
3. ________ you from? I'm from Medellin, Colombia.
4. ________ your birthday? It's July 3.
5. ________ your favorite singer? Ariana Grande.

16–20 correct: You can talk about greetings and ordinal numbers. You can use *be* statements and information questions.
0–15 correct: Look again at the Vocabulary and Grammar sections in the unit.

TOTAL SCORE: / 20

WHAT DO YOU KNOW NOW? Look back at page 7 and add the words you know now to the box.

STUDY SKILLS MEMORY STRATEGIES

Take the quiz about memory strategies. Go to **Study Skills** on page 127 to find the answers. Then learn more about memory strategies.

1 Left-handed people have better memories.
a true **b** false

2 Which foods help your memory?
a chicken and potatoes **b** vegetables, fruit, and nuts **c** cheese and chocolate

3 What is a good way to help you remember things?
a Sleep after studying. **b** Exercise before studying. **c** Drink coffee when you study.

4 It is possible for students to learn … new words per hour of study.
a 1–5 **b** 5–10 **c** 10–20

UNIT 2

Work/Life Balance

WHAT DO YOU ALREADY KNOW?

1 Think about your day and the things you do at school or work, with family, and with friends. Write the activities and the percentage of time you do the activities each week.

2 IN PAIRS Share and compare your activities. Think of more words to add to each category.

School or work __%

Family __%

Friends __%

VIDEO

DISCUSS & SHARE

3 IN GROUPS Watch the video and answer the question.

SYM Is it possible to have a good work and life balance?

In this unit, you will ...

- talk about jobs, members of your family, and what jobs they do.
- use thinking skills: hypothesize, infer, and categorize.
- read about a young woman entrepreneur.
- use strategies to repair talking by checking for understanding.
- use notes when you speak in front of the class.
- use self-awareness skills to evaluate your interests and abilities for a job.
- follow an IT professional to learn about this job and the skills needed for this industry.

READING

A **Are you (or a member of your family) a business owner? What business is it? Discuss.**

B 2.01 **Read the article. Then discuss the questions.**

A Woman at Work Zinah Saleh, Iraq

Zinah Saleh is a **business owner** with a **successful** business. She is the owner of her **company**, Ishtar Handmade Soap. Her company makes eco-friendly soap and shampoo. The all-natural soap **products** are very popular. All of the products use olive oil from Iraq. They also use fruit from trees in Africa.

Female business owners are unusual in Iraq. Zinah has a degree in business administration, and she wants to help women find jobs. Zinah's **employees** are all women. There are female soap makers, **administrators**, and **marketers**. Zinah's parents are happy for her. Her father is an engineer and her mother is a homemaker. Zinah thinks working women are important for her country's economy.

Read more

1 Where is Zinah Saleh from?
2 What is her job?
3 What is Zinah's business?
4 What is in the Ishtar products?
5 What is unusual about Zinah's company?

C READING SKILL—Scan **Read the article quickly and underline the jobs.**

D THINKING SKILL—Question **Why do you think eco-friendly products are popular? Are eco-friendly products important to you? Discuss.**

VOCABULARY

A **Find words from the article that match the definitions. Write the word.**

1 another word for business ____________
2 people who advertise products ____________
3 people who work for a business owner ____________
4 people who manage the paperwork of a business ____________
5 a person who has a business ____________
6 things that a business sells ____________

B **List eight adjectives from the article.**

____________ ____________ ____________ ____________
____________ ____________ ____________ ____________

GRAMMAR articles *a, an,* and no article

A **Choose the correct option to complete the rules.**

1 The words *a* and *an* come before **singular** / **plural** nouns.
2 *A* comes before a noun that starts with a **vowel** / **consonant**.
3 *An* comes before a noun that starts with a **vowel** / **consonant**.
4 In adjective + noun phrases, *a/an* comes before the **adjective** / **noun**.
5 If a noun is plural, use ***a*** / ***an*** / **no article**.

For more practice, go to page 143.

B **Complete with *a*, *an*, or *X* (no article).**

1 _____ homemaker is an important job.
2 There are _____ social media marketers at online companies.
3 I think business owners have _____ exciting jobs.
4 A lot of women in my country are _____ business owners.
5 I prefer _____ creative job, like _____ art teacher or _____ music teacher.
6 Math is important to be _____ engineer or _____ architect.

MAKE IT YOURS

Make a list of local businesses in your area. What products or services do the businesses sell?

C **IN PAIRS** **Read the sentences in B. Are they true, in your opinion?**

PRONUNCIATION *an* + vowel

A **2.02 Listen and notice how phrases with *an* sound like /æ/ + a word beginning with *n*. Practice saying the words. Draw a line to connect *an* to the vowel of the next word.**

an architect	an economist	an interior designer	an office manager
an art teacher	an engineer	an interpreter	an optometrist

SPEAKING

A **Make a list of facts you know about a famous person in your notebook.**

B **IN GROUPS** **Ask questions and guess who the famous person is. Use the Confident Communicator box to help you.**

A: Is it a man or a woman? — *B: A …*
A: How old is he/she? — *B: I think he/she's about …*
A: When is his/her birthday? — *B: I don't know.*
A: Where's he/she from? — *B: He/She's from …*
A: Is he/she married? — *B: I think so. / I don't know.*
A: What does he/she do? — *B: He's/She's a/an …*
A: Is it … ? — *B: Yes, it is! / No, it isn't!*

CONFIDENT COMMUNICATOR

KEEP TALKING

If you don't know the answer to a question, say:
I don't know.
If you think you know an answer, but you are not sure, say:
I (don't) think so. / I think it's/she's/he's …

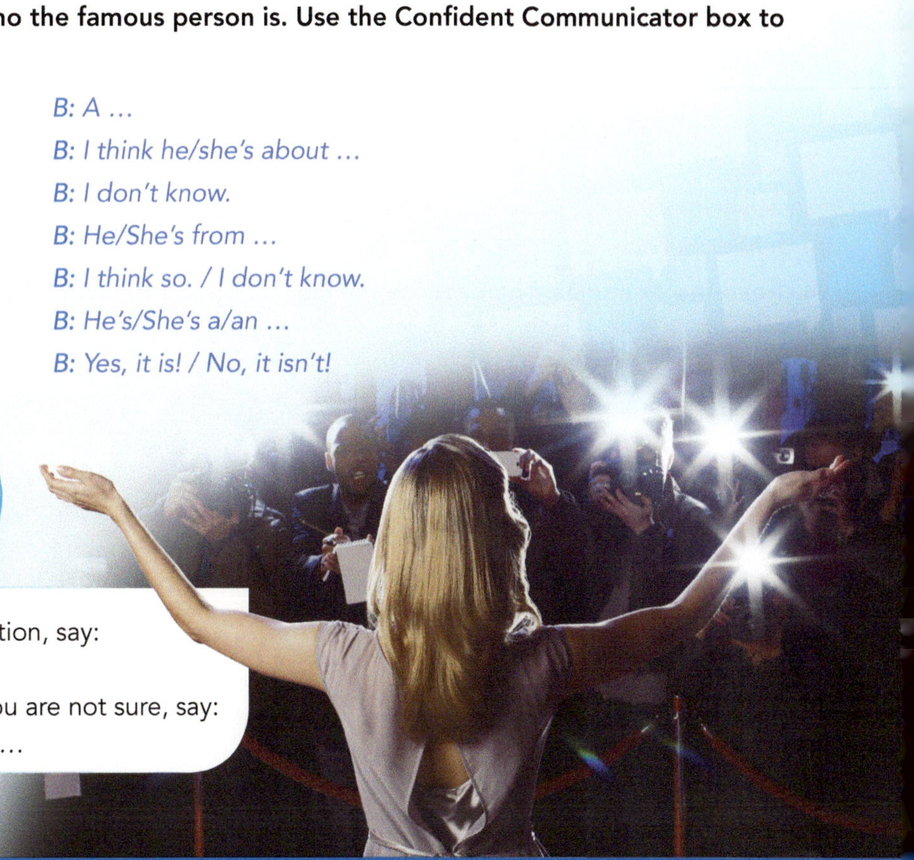

Family Connections

VOCABULARY family

A Complete Sherry's family tree with words from the box.

aunt brother cousin mother nephew niece son uncle

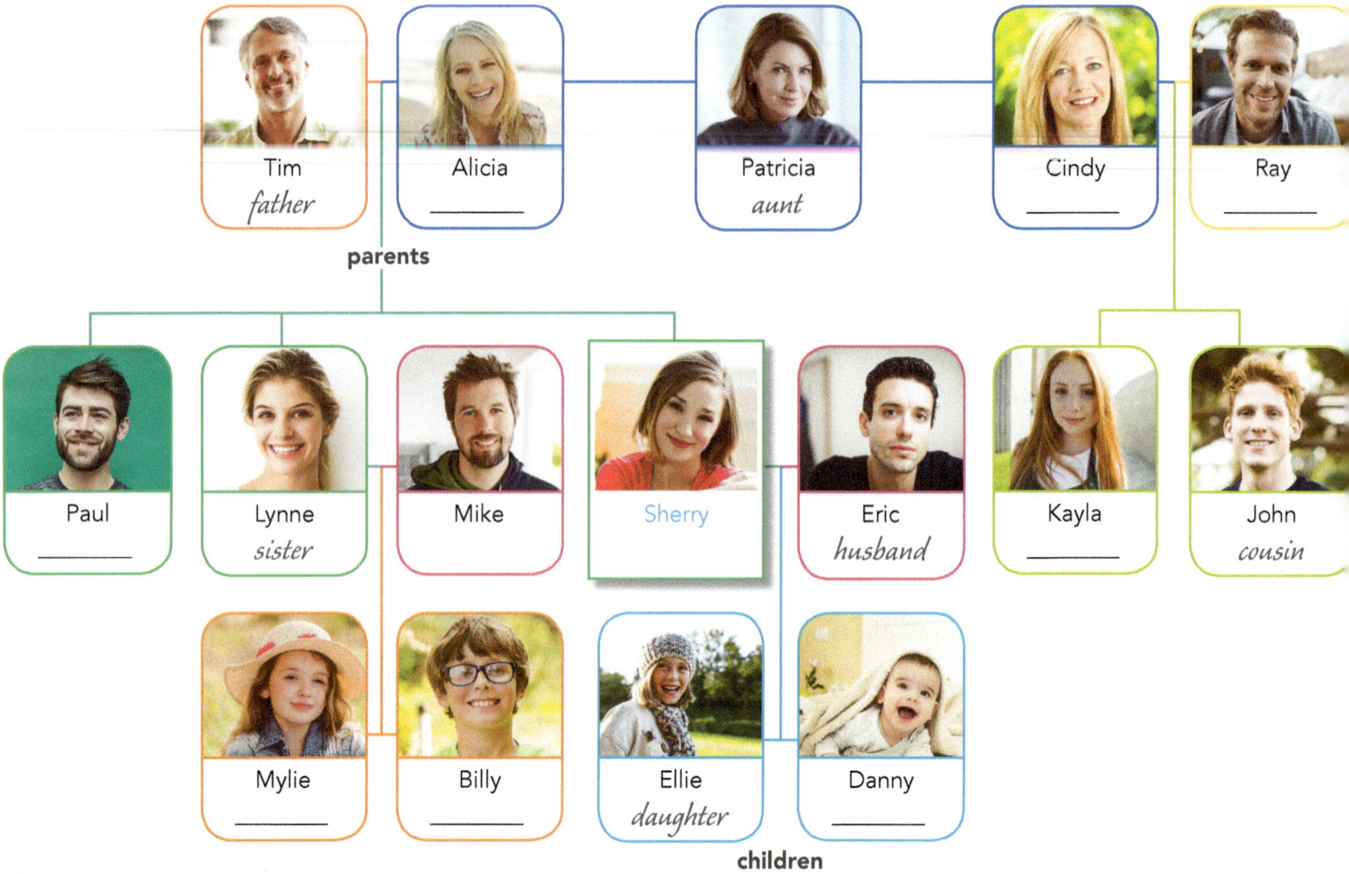

B 2.03 Listen and check your answers.

MAKE IT REAL

People often use different words for immediate family members.

father: *dad, pa, pop, daddy* mother: *mom, mama, ma, mommy*
brother: *bro* sister: *sis*

GRAMMAR possessive adjectives and *'s/s'*

A Read the examples. Then choose the correct option to complete the rules.

Tim is **Sherry's** father.
Her children's names are Ellie and Danny.
Her **parents'** names are Tim and Alicia.
Whose sister is Sherry? She's Paul's and Lynne's sister.
Ellie and Danny are children. **Their** parents are Sherry and Eric.

Eric is married to **his** wife, Sherry.
Sherry has a sister. **Her** name is Lynne.

1 Show possession with *'s* for **singular or irregular** / **plural** nouns.
2 Show possession with *s'* for **singular** / **plural** nouns.
3 When you refer to a man, use the possessive adjective ***his*** / ***her*** / ***their***.
4 When you refer to a woman, use the possessive adjective ***his*** / ***her*** / ***their***.
5 When you refer to two or more people, use the possessive adjective ***his*** / ***her*** / ***their***.
6 Use ***Whose*** / ***Who*** to ask how two people are connected in the family.

For more practice, go to page 144.

B Find and correct one error in each sentence.

Her ~~fathers~~ *father's* name is Tim.

1 Sherrys' mother's name is Alicia.

2 Her parent's hometown is Chicago.

3 Who's children are Danny and Ellie? They're Sherry's children.

4 Ray is Cindy's husband. Our children are Kayla and John.

5 Sherry's children's names' are Danny and Ellie.

C IN PAIRS Ask each other questions about Sherry's family tree.

A: Whose husband is Eric? *B: He's Sherry's husband.*

LISTENING

A IN PAIRS Look at the family picture. Guess how the people are connected to Alan.

B 2.04 LISTENING SKILL—Use visual clues Listen to Alan talk about the picture and complete.

1 Mary is Alan's ______________.
2 Kaitlyn is Kevin's ______________.
3 Kevin is Alan's ______________. He's ______________ to Kaitlyn.
4 Linda is Alan's ______________. Her ______________ is Steve.
5 Mindy is Alan's niece. Her ______________ is Mary.
6 Robert isn't ______________. He's ______________ years old.

C IN PAIRS THINKING SKILL—Analyze Discuss the questions.

1 What is Sarah's relationship to Alan?
2 Does Sarah know Alan's family?
3 Why does Alan say, "Of course, Robert isn't married"?

SPEAKING

A Draw your family tree in your notebook. Fill in some of the names, but leave the others blank.

B IN PAIRS Ask questions to complete your partner's family tree. Then look at your family tree and correct errors. Use the Confident Communicator box to help you.

A: What's your aunt's name? *B: Her name is Anna. Her husband is Frank.*

CONFIDENT COMMUNICATOR
REPAIR IT

Names can be difficult to understand. Ask questions to check your understanding.
Can you repeat his/her name?
How do you spell that?

LESSON 3 Jobs

VOCABULARY jobs

A **IN GROUPS** **Make a list of jobs you know in your notebook.**

B **Match the pictures to the jobs from the box. Write the words under each picture.**

accountant	architect	computer technician	interpreter
journalist	nurse	pharmacist	pilot

LISTENING

A **LISTENING SKILL—Predict** **Look at the family picture. What do you think Molly will talk about?**

MAKE IT YOURS

Make a list of the jobs your family members have. Include your job or the job you want to have in the future. Use your dictionary if necessary.

B **2.05 Listen and answer the questions.**

1 Who's in the picture? *Molly's aunt,*
2 Where are they?
3 How old is Jeff?
4 What is Jeff's job?
5 What is Elsa's job?
6 What is Pete's job?
7 How old is Laurie?

C **THINKING SKILL—Categorize** **Discuss the questions.**

1 What jobs in this lesson are associated with math ability, science ability, or creative ability?
2 What jobs require a university degree?

WRITING

A Complete the family profile using information from the table.

	Person 1	Person 2	Person 3	Person 4
Relationship to you	father	mother	uncle	sister
Age	65	58	60	25
Job	engineer	accountant	math teacher	manager
Place of work	retired	New Systems	Lincoln High School	a restaurant

MY PROFILE

MY FAMILY

The members of my family have interesting jobs. My dad is a/an **1** ____________, but he's **2** ____________ and he's retired now. My **3** ____________ is 58, and she's an accountant at **4** ____________. It's an IT company. My Uncle Joe is a **5** ____________ at Lincoln High School. He's my dad's brother. My sister is only **6** ____________, but she's the manager of a large restaurant.

B Complete the table for your family.

	Family Member 1: ________	Family Member 2: ________	Family Member 3: ________	Family Member 4: ________
Relationship to you				
Age				
Job				
Place of work				

C Write your family profile in your notebook.

D IN PAIRS Read and discuss your family profiles. Correct grammar, spelling, and punctuation.

SPEAKING

A Prepare to talk about your favorite family picture and make notes in your notebook. Use the Confident Communicator box to help you.

1. Who's in the picture and what is their relationship to you?
2. Where are the people in the picture?
3. What are their relationships to other family members (for example, *my mother's sister*)?
4. How old are they?
5. What do they do?

B IN GROUPS Share and discuss your picture.

My favorite picture is of me, my sister, and our cousins Ronny and Jenny. Ronny is a computer programmer. Jenny is …

CONFIDENT COMMUNICATOR

KEEP TALKING

When you use notes to help you talk about something, look quickly at your notes, but don't read them aloud.

Language and Life

Self-awareness – The Right Job

A 2.06 **Read the Careers Profile and the job ads, then answer the question in your notebook.**

Which two jobs fit David's interests and abilities?

CAREERS PROFILE	**Name:** David Monetti			
For each category, choose two areas that describe your interests and abilities.				
Personality	☐ organized	☑ friendly	☐ patient	☑ independent
Natural abilities	☑ verbal	☑ logical/ mathematical	☐ creative	☐ social
Academic skills	☐ science and math	☑ language	☑ technology	☐ arts

CAREERS PROFILE Results

High school English teacher

Job description: Teach grammar, writing, and literature. Patience, good communication skills, and IT/social media skills are necessary.

Journalist for city newspaper

Job description: Talk to people and write stories. Need good English and computer skills. We want a creative, independent person.

Computer technician for large company

Job description: Work with computers and help people with computer problems. Lots of travel. A science and engineering education is required.

Marketer for small communications company

Job description: Need a friendly, creative, social person. Good computer and social media skills are necessary. Art or design education is not necessary, but good writing is very important.

B **IN PAIRS** **Compare your ideas and discuss.**

A: I think the right jobs for David are English teacher and journalist. His verbal and language skills are good.

B: Maybe journalist, but not English teacher. He isn't patient.

C **IN GROUPS** **Complete with the kind of personality, abilities, and skills you need for each job.**

1 accountant: *organized,* ______________________
2 nurse: ______________________
3 journalist: ______________________
4 engineer: ______________________
5 designer: ______________________

D **Complete a Careers Profile for you.**

CAREERS PROFILE | **Name:**

For each category, choose two areas that describe your interests and abilities.

Personality	☐ organized	☐ friendly	☐ patient	☐ independent
Natural abilities	☐ verbal	☐ logical/ mathematical	☐ creative	☐ social
Academic skills	☐ science and math	☐ language	☐ technology	☐ arts

E **Complete a list of jobs and skills for you.**

Possible jobs

Job:

Skills I have for the job:

Job:

Skills I have for the job:

Job:

Skills I have for the job:

F **IN GROUPS** **Share your lists of jobs and skills. Discuss and make suggestions.**

A: What about an architect? Your logic and math skills are good, and you're creative.

B: Or a math teacher. You're patient.

MAKE IT DIGITAL

Go online and look for job listings in your area. Think about which jobs are good for you, based on your interests and abilities.

VOCABULARY review

SCORE: / 10

A Choose the correct option to complete the sentences about Elena's family.

My **1 mother** / **father** is very creative. She's an art **2 engineer** / **teacher**. My mother's sister Ana is my **3 aunt** / **cousin**. Her house is beautiful. She's an **4 accountant** / **interior designer**. Nina is Ana's daughter. She's my **5 sister** / **cousin**. When I have a laptop problem, I call her. She's a **6 computer technician** / **marketer**. My **7 father** / **daughter** works for a large company. His name is Ricardo. He speaks English and Portuguese. He's an **8 interpreter** / **office manager**. My **9 grandfather** / **uncle** is my father's father. He sells computers. He's a small business **10 owner** / **optometrist**.

GRAMMAR review

SCORE: / 10

A Complete the job ad with *a*, *an*, or *X* (no article).

Do you want **1** _____ interesting job? Think about a job as **2** _____ social media manager. **3** _____ social media manager writes **4** _____ comments and connects with **5** _____ customers. Contact us at our website to apply.

B Complete the sentences with words from the box.

's s' his her their

1 My parent ____________ names are Mark and Cindy.
2 My sister is named Kathy, but ____________ nickname is Kat.
3 My brother ____________ name is Jeff.
4 He's married to ____________ wife, Ann.
5 ____________ daughter's name is Barbara.

16–20 correct: You can talk about family and jobs. You can use *a*/*an* and the verb *be*.
0–15 correct: Look again at the Vocabulary and Grammar sections in the unit.

TOTAL SCORE: / 20

WHAT DO YOU KNOW NOW? Look back at page 17 and add the words you know now to the boxes.

FOLLOW A PRO INFORMATION TECHNOLOGY (IT)

Take the quiz about IT (information technology). Go to **Follow A Pro** on page 128 to find the answers. Then learn more about the IT industry.

1 Which country has the most internet users?
a China **b** the UK **c** the US

2 How many new viruses go into the internet every month?
a 360 **b** 6,000 **c** 10,000

3 Why is November 30 a special day? It's ...
a clean your computer day. **b** internet safety day. **c** computer security day.

4 What percentage of internet traffic is web robots?
a 8% **b** 55% **c** 21%

UNIT 3 Fun and Games

WHAT DO YOU ALREADY KNOW?

1 **Think of words you know about free-time activities. Write activities that you can do indoors and outdoors.**

2 **IN PAIRS** **Share and compare your activities. Add more words to your lists.**

Outdoor activities
play tennis

Indoor activities
play music

VIDEO

DISCUSS & SHARE

3 **IN GROUPS** **Watch the video and answer the question.**

SYM How much time do you need alone or with other people?

In this unit, you will ...

- express likes and dislikes, recommend free-time activities, and talk about an event.
- use thinking skills: categorize, infer, and recall.
- read a magazine interview.
- use strategies to keep talking and emphasize preferences, giving reasons, and expressing rules.
- use creativity skills to work with others and create an interest group for a website.
- learn tips for a successful oral presentation.

Like It, Love It, or Hate It?

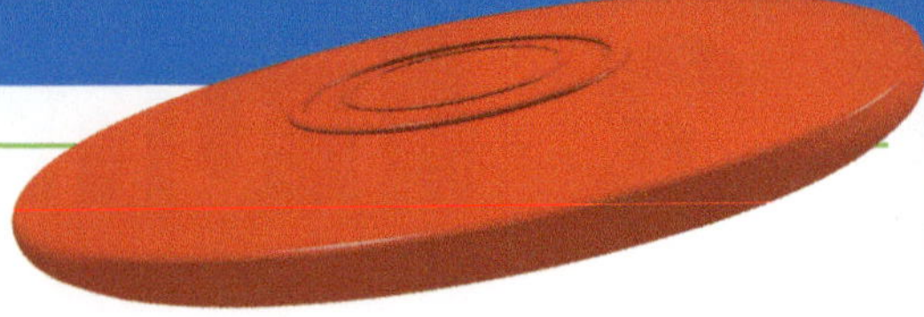

READING

A IN GROUPS Discuss free-time activities. What do you like doing in your free time? Which type of activity is the most popular in your group?

B 3.01 READING SKILL—Infer Read the magazine interview and answer the question. Who is Otto?

NEW FRISBEE CHAMPIONS!

Here is an interview with Chris Watson, one half of the Chris-Otto Frisbee team. Chris and Otto are this year's winners.

Interviewer: Congratulations, Chris! You and Otto are the winners! Do you have time to talk to me?

Chris: Sure, thanks. Otto is a great Frisbee player! He runs really fast, and he always catches the Frisbee. Otto loves Frisbee, too. We practice together every day.

Interviewer: Does he like other outdoor activities?

Chris: Well, yes, he likes hiking, but he doesn't like hiking in cold weather.

Interviewer: Does he have any special likes or dislikes?

Chris: Yes, he does. He loves watching TV. He watches soccer and football with me a lot. I like golf, but Otto thinks it's boring. I don't watch it often. And … let's see. He likes eating—a lot! And he hates cats!

Interviewer: Thanks, Chris. Good luck to you and Otto next season.

Chris: Thanks.

Otto: Woof!

C THINKING SKILL—Categorize Read the interview again and write Otto's likes and dislikes in the table.

Otto likes …	Otto doesn't like …

VOCABULARY

A Read the verbs and complete the sentences for you. Discuss with a partner.

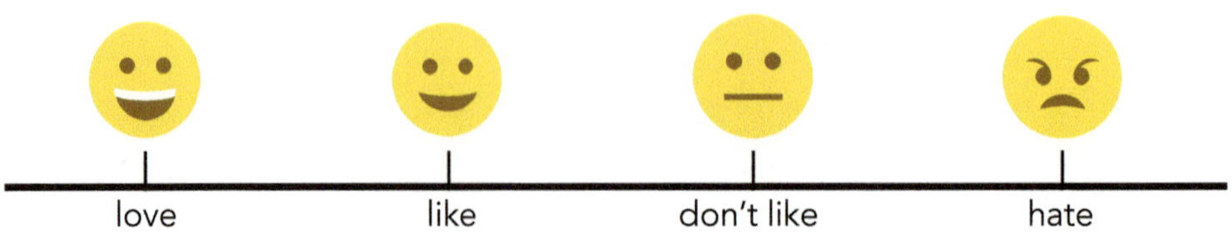

1 I ______________ sports.
2 I ______________ romantic movies.
3 I ______________ hiking.
4 I ______________ playing video games.
5 I ______________ using social media.
6 I ______________ listening to music.

GRAMMAR simple present statements and *yes/no* questions

A Read the examples from the interview. Then choose the correct option to complete the rules.

He loves watching sports on TV.
I like golf.
I don't watch it often.

He doesn't like hiking in cold weather.
Do you have time to talk to me? Yes, I do.
Does he have any special likes or dislikes? Yes, he does.

1. For statements with *I*, *you*, *we*, and *they*, add / don't add an *–s* to the verb.
2. For statements with *he*, *she*, and *it*, add / don't add an *–s* to the verb.
3. The correct word order for *yes/no* questions is *Do* or *Does* + subject + verb / Subject + *do* or *does* + verb.
4. Short answers to *yes/no* questions end in *do* or *does* / a verb.

For more practice, go to page 145.

B Choose the correct option.

1. Do / Does you like soccer? Yes, I like. / Yes, I do.
2. I love / loves tennis, but my brother isn't / doesn't like it.
3. Do / Does your dad like watching sports on TV? No, he don't / doesn't.
4. My sister and I love / loves video games, but my brother doesn't like / likes them.
5. He play / plays games on his phone, but I think / thinks games are boring.

MAKE IT REAL

Alternative phrases for short answers:
A: Do you like swimming?
B: Not really. / No, but I like … / It's OK. / Sure. / Of course.

C IN PAIRS Discuss preferences.

A: Do you like basketball? *B: I like watching it, but I don't like playing it.*
A: Do you like playing soccer? *B: Yes, I do. I like watching it, too!*

PRONUNCIATION third person *–s*

A 3.02 Listen and notice the final sound of each word. Practice saying the words.

Sounds like /s/: likes, hates, walks, thinks
Sounds like /z/: loves, swims, plays, runs
Sounds like /iz/: watches, uses, practices, catches

B IN PAIRS Practice reading aloud. Pronounce the verbs correctly.

1. Otto runs fast, and he always catches the Frisbee.
2. My brother loves tennis. He practices every day.
3. My sister thinks hiking is boring, but she likes swimming.
4. My dad hates social media, but he uses it for his business.

SPEAKING

A Make a list of free-time activities that you like in your notebook.

B IN PAIRS Discuss what you like and don't like. Draw faces next to the activities on your list according to your partner's answers.

A: Do you like playing video games? *B: No, I hate it!*

C IN GROUPS Find another pair. Tell them about your partner's preferences. Use the Confident Communicator box to help you.

Mark hates playing video games, but he likes playing cards.

CONFIDENT COMMUNICATOR — KEEP TALKING

Add words to give more information about your preferences.
*I **really** like/hate swimming.*
*I don't like swimming **very much**.*
*I like swimming **a lot**.*

LESSON 2 Preferences

VOCABULARY free-time activities

A Complete the table with words from the box.

audiobooks shopping dancing soccer ~~movies~~ to eat music TV online videos video games parties with friends ~~podcasts~~ ~~the movies~~

listen to	watch	play	go	go to	go out
podcasts	*movies*			*the movies*	

B IN GROUPS Discuss whether you like or don't like the same things.

A: Do you like listening to music or to podcasts? I prefer music.
B: Music.
C: Music.
D: Podcasts.
A: OK, three for music and one for podcasts.

MAKE IT YOURS

List other free-time activities that you like to do or places that you like to go to.

LISTENING

A As a class, list some of your favorite games, movies, musicians, and TV shows.

games ____________

movies ____________

musicians ____________

TV shows ____________

B 3.03 Listen to the phone conversation and answer the question. What is the event?

C 3.03 LISTENING SKILL—Take notes Listen again and complete the notes.

Event:
Date:
Time:
Place:
Ticket price:

D 3.03 THINKING SKILL—Understand Listen again and choose the correct option.

1 Who buys the tickets?
a Rob **b** Sandy **c** Rob and Sandy

2 Who pays for the tickets?
a Rob **b** Sandy **c** Rob and Sandy

GRAMMAR the imperative

A Read the examples from the conversation and choose the correct option to complete the rules.

Listen to this!
Please get me a ticket!
Don't forget to write down the information.
Tell me the date again, please.

1 We use the imperative to ...
 a give opinions. b give orders or instructions. c talk about likes and dislikes.
2 The verb form in imperative sentences is ...
 a base form. b *to* + verb. c verb + *–ing*.
3 To form a negative imperative, use ...
 a verb + *not*. b *doesn't* + verb. c *don't* + verb.
4 For a polite imperative, add *please* ... of the sentence.
 a at the beginning b at the end c at the beginning or end

For more practice, go to page 146.

B Complete the conversation with verbs from the box.

don't buy forget listen tell turn use

Erika: **1** __________ to this new song by Logan Williams.
Laura: It's great! **2** __________ up the volume!
Erika: Here. **3** __________ my headphones.
Laura: Excellent! What's the name of the song?
Erika: "Party Night." The song is great, but **4** __________ the album. The other songs aren't very good.
Laura: OK. Hey, **5** __________ to get that new app. It's really good.
Erika: Oh, yeah. **6** __________ me the name again, please.
Laura: It's called *Guess Who*.

C IN PAIRS Role-play the conversation in B with a singer, song, and app that you like.

SPEAKING

A Complete the table with things you like and don't like. Add two more things to the list of activities.

Activities	Like	Don't Like
Movies		
Apps		
Books		
TV shows		

B IN GROUPS Give recommendations. Use the Confident Communicator box to help you.

CONFIDENT COMMUNICATOR
KEEP TALKING

When you give a negative recommendation, try to give a reason.
OK, for movies, go see the new Spielberg movie. It's excellent.
Don't see Mystery on the Beach. It's terrible/boring/silly/violent.

LESSON 3 Special Events

LISTENING

A Think about the words in the box and discuss the questions.

concerts festivals sports events other types of competitions

1 Which special events happen in your area?
2 What type of event is your favorite?

B 3.04 LISTENING SKILL—Listen for gist Listen and choose the correct option.

1 What type of recording is this?
 a a TV program **b** an advertisement **c** a podcast
2 What is the speaker talking about?
 a a festival **b** a concert **c** a race

C 3.04 Listen again and choose *True* or *False*.

1 This is a national festival. True / False
2 The festival includes two races. True / False
3 The soccer players are children. True / False
4 The festival is open eight hours every day. True / False
5 The festival doesn't welcome pets. True / False
6 Buy your tickets at the festival to get a discount. True / False

D THINKING SKILL—Recall Write and compare.

1 Make a list of the events from the advertisement. With a partner, compare your lists and add to them.

VOCABULARY special events

A Write two words from the box in each column.

baseball motorcycle pop photography hip hop singing horse soccer

a ... concert	a ... game	a ... race	a ... competition
rock	football	10-km	cooking
classical	basketball	bicycle	dance

B Complete the sentences for you.

1 I love ______________ concerts.
2 I think ______________ races are dangerous.
3 I don't like ______________ competitions.
4 I love to watch ______________ games.
5 I like going to ______________ festivals.

MAKE IT YOURS

What types of local or special events are in your area? Add more events to the lists in **A**.

C IN GROUPS Discuss your opinions.

A: I love rock concerts.
B: Me, too.
C: I prefer pop concerts.

WRITING

A Read the poster and label with words from the box.

date	description of event	name of event	place
a recommendation	ticket information	time	rules

1 ____________
2 ____________
3 ____________
4 ____________
5 ____________
6 ____________
7 ____________
8 ____________

B IN GROUPS Plan a poster for an event in your area.

EVENT PLANNING FORM

Name and/or type of event ____________
Specific information about the event ____________
Place ____________
Date ____________
Starting/Ending times ____________
Ticket information ____________
Rules ____________
Recommendation ____________
Other information ____________

C Create your poster. Emphasize important information and make your poster attractive.

SPEAKING

A IN GROUPS Describe the event from your poster. Use the Confident Communicator box to help you.

A: The event is … *B: The rules are …*
A: It's in/near … *B: My favorite thing is … / I don't recommend the …*

B Share with the class. Show your poster and describe the event.

C Take a class vote. What poster do you like best? What event do you want to go to?

CONFIDENT COMMUNICATOR
KEEP TALKING

Ways to express rules:
No dogs/food/backpacks *Children over 12 only*
Pets/food/drinks are OK *Drinks only; no food*

Language and Life

Creativity – An Interest Group

A 3.05 **Read the social media web page. Then choose the correct option below.**

GET TOGETHER

Name of group: Music Lovers join

Do you love music? Do you sing or play an instrument? This is the group for you! We like to go to concerts together, but we LOVE to make our own music!

Name of group: Latinos Play join

We are a group of students from Latin American countries. We like eating food from our countries and meeting other Latin American students here in Los Angeles. If you speak Spanish and love good food, join our group!

Upcoming Meetings

Attend	Attend	Attend
15 SEP — Sat. Sep 15, 7… Music Lovers, Thompson Park	15 SEP — Sat. Sep 15, 9… Latinos Play Public library	16 SEP — Sun. Sep 16, 8… Biking Club, Riverside Park
15 going	8 going	12 going

How to join Get Together

Register for free. Then click on your interests and read about local groups. The members of the groups meet and do different activities. Join the groups that interest you.

How to create a Get Together group

You can start your own Get Together group. Click on "Create a Group." Enter your location. Click on your interest for the new group. Choose a title for the group. Write a short profile of the group. Click "Create Group."

CREATE A GROUP

1 People use this website to …
   a take classes to learn new hobbies. **b** meet new friends with similar interests. **c** meet people to date.
2 The members of the first group like to …
   a listen to music. **b** play music. **c** listen to and play music.
3 The members of the second group are all from …
   a Latin America. **b** Los Angeles. **c** the same country.

B **IN PAIRS Read the social media post. Then discuss.**

1 What is Miguel's problem?
2 Are either of the two groups in **A** right for him?

Language Institute Blog

miguel Posted SEP 17 7:06 p.m.

My name is Miguel, and I'm from Ecuador. I study English in a language institute in Los Angeles. I want to meet new friends with similar interests and practice my English. I like hiking, concerts, and good food. My favorite foods are Italian and Chinese food. Please give me some ideas.

follow

C **IN PAIRS** Choose Miguel's interests to help him create a new Get Together group.

GET TOGETHER

NEW GROUP

Location: Los Angeles, CA
Interests

watching sports ♡ playing team sports ♡ hiking ♡ dancing ♡ biking ♡

dating ♡ pets ♡ food & restaurants ♡ cooking ♡ international students ♡

concerts ♡ musicians ♡ movies ♡ theater ♡ gaming ♡

D Choose one of Miguel's interests from C and create a new group.

GET TOGETHER

NEW GROUP

Location: Los Angeles, CA
Interests

Interest area:

Name of group:

Description of group:

E Take a class vote. Read your description of Miguel's interest group and decide which new interest group is best for him.

F **IN GROUPS** Discuss.

1 Do you know of any websites like Get Together in your area?
2 Do you use a website like Get Together? If so, what groups do you belong to?
3 What are your interests? Do you want to join a website like Get Together?

MAKE IT DIGITAL

Start a network of interest groups in your school or institute to meet people with similar interests and practice your English.

VOCABULARY review

SCORE: / 10

A Match the sentence beginning (1–10) to the sentence end (a–j). Write the letter.

1 Dani likes to read books and listen to ____
2 Sally loves to dance and go to ____
3 Erik likes to watch ____
4 Hannah loves to play ____
5 Rich loves to go ____
6 Pedro likes to go out ____
7 Yumiko likes to run and play ____
8 Marta likes to go for ____
9 Isobel and her friends love to use ____
10 My dog hates to take ____

a games on her phone.
b shopping and spend money.
c audiobooks.
d parties with friends.
e movies at home on his big TV.
f a bath.
g walks in the park.
h social media.
i tennis.
j to eat in restaurants.

GRAMMAR review

SCORE: / 10

A Choose the correct option.

Berta: Hi, Frida! I'm in the online Music Interest Group with you. **1** Do you play / Do you plays more than one musical instrument?
Frida: Yes, I **2** am / do. Drums and piano! I **3** practice / practices every day. My parents **4** don't like / doesn't like the drums! I'm in the school band. **5** Does your school have / Do your school have a band?
Berta: No, it **6** doesn't / don't. But there's a music and dance club.
Frida: **7** Do you dance / Does you dance well?
Berta: No, I **8** don't / doesn't. Oh, I have to go to class!
Frida: OK. Please **9** Text / text again soon. **10** Not forget / Don't forget to post a picture! Here's a picture of me!

16–20 correct: You can talk about likes, dislikes, and free-time activities. You can use the simple present and *yes/no* questions.
0–15 correct: Look again at the Vocabulary and Grammar sections in the unit.

TOTAL SCORE: / 20

WHAT DO YOU KNOW NOW? Look back at page 27 and add the words you know now to the boxes.

STUDY SKILLS ORAL PRESENTATIONS

Take the quiz about oral presentations. Go to **Study Skills** on page 129 to find the answers. Then learn more about oral presentations.

1 You need to spend 50% of your time writing your presentation.
a true **b** false

2 When people see pictures, they remember … of what they hear and see.
a 60% **b** 80% **c** 95%

3 You want to begin your talk. What do you say?
a "Please listen to me." **b** "Silence!" **c** "Hello. Today I'm talking about …"

4 You want to finish your talk. What do you say?
a "That's all." **b** "Thank you for listening. Any questions?" **c** "The end!"

UNIT
4 That's Life!

WHAT DO YOU ALREADY KNOW?

1 **Think of words about the activities you do every day. Write the words for the activities.**

2 **IN PAIRS** **Share and compare your information. Add more words to your lists.**

Planned Activities
eat breakfast

Unexpected Things
get sick

VIDEO

DISCUSS & SHARE

3 **IN GROUPS** **Watch the video and answer the question.**

SYM Do you plan your day or decide what to do at the last minute?

In this unit, you will ...

- talk about daily activities and how often you do them. Describe a day off.
- use thinking skills: draw conclusions, summarize, and recall.
- read about a reporter's typical day.
- use strategies to start and keep talking by giving examples and expressing frequency.
- use adaptability skills to give advice about keeping life interesting.
- follow an emergency worker to learn about this job and the skills needed for this industry.

A Day in the Life

READING

A **Take a class survey. How many people think their lives are boring, average, or exciting?**

B 4.01 THINKING SKILL—Analyze **Read the blog post. In your opinion, is Jerry's life boring, average, or exciting?**

The Daily Blog

Jan 21 1:43 p.m.

A Day in the Life of a Reporter

I'm a reporter. I work for an entertainment magazine in New York City. My friends think my job is amazing because I meet famous people. But this is my typical day.

I get up at about 6:30 a.m., and then I **walk my dog**, **have coffee**, and **get ready for work**. I leave home at 7:15 a.m., and I **take the subway** to my office. I **start work** at 8:00 a.m. I don't eat breakfast at home because I don't have time. I buy something at the café in the subway station. At work, I go to meetings and write articles for the magazine. I also **make** a lot of **phone calls** to get interviews with people. The interviews are interesting, but sometimes the people I interview aren't very friendly or they don't have time to talk.

In the evening, I **go home** and walk my dog again. Then, I **have dinner** and watch TV for about two hours. I go to bed at about 10:00 p.m. On weekends, I go out with friends, go shopping, or go to a movie.

follow

C IN PAIRS READING SKILL—Scan **Find the answers as quickly as possible.**

1 What time does Jerry get up?
2 Where does he live?
3 Why do his friends think his job is amazing?
4 How does he get to work?
5 Who does he go out with on weekends?

VOCABULARY

A **Find words from the blog post that match the definitions. Write the word.**

1 begin your workday: ____________
2 exercise with your dog: ____________
3 drink coffee: ____________
4 prepare for work: ____________
5 travel by subway: ____________
6 call people: ____________
7 return to your home: ____________
8 eat dinner: ____________

GRAMMAR simple present information questions

A **Complete the questions with words from the box.**

how what when where who why

Information Questions: Question Word + *Do/Does* + Subject + Verb / Verb Phrase	
1 ____________ do your parents do?	They're teachers.
2 ____________ does your brother work?	He works at a bank.
3 ____________ does he work?	He works from Monday to Friday.
4 ____________ do you like your job?	I like it because it's very interesting.
5 ____________ do you get to work?	I take the bus.
6 ____________ do you see on weekends?	I see my best friend.

For more practice, go to page 146.

B **Unscramble the questions.**

1 do / on weekends / you / what / do / ?

____

2 in your free time / who / you / do / see / ?

____

3 go / you / where / on vacation / do / ?

____

4 English / you / study / do / why / ?

____

5 do / when / you / your English homework / do / ?

____

6 to English class / you / do / get / how / ?

____

C IN PAIRS **Ask and answer the questions in B.**

PRONUNCIATION word stress in information questions

A 4.02 **Listen and underline the stressed words.**

1 What do you do?
2 Where do you live?
3 Why do you like your job?
4 When do you go on vacation?
5 How do you get to class?

B 4.02 **Listen again. Practice reading the questions with the correct word stress.**

SPEAKING

A **Use the cues to write interview questions.**

1 What / do?

____

2 Where / work or study?

____

3 When / have English class?

____

4 How / get to work?

____

5 What time / start work?

____

6 What / do in your free time?

____

B IN PAIRS **Interview your partner. Write his/her answers in A.**

C IN GROUPS **Is your life boring, average, or exciting? Are your partners' lives exciting? Use the Confident Communicator box to help you.**

CONFIDENT COMMUNICATOR
START TALKING

To describe your life, give examples to support your opinion using *because*.
My life is exciting because I travel a lot / meet a lot of interesting people / have a great social life.
My life is average because I like my job, but it isn't exciting / I just do normal things.
My life is boring because my job isn't interesting / I don't do many interesting things / I do the same things every day.

Always? Sometimes? Never?

LISTENING

A **As a class, discuss jobs you think are exciting.**

B 4.03 **Listen to an interview with an actress. Does she think her life is exciting? Why or why not?**

MAKE IT REAL

Really means *very*: *That's really early.*
Some Americans say *real* for *really*: *That's real early.*
Kind of means *a little*: *My job is kind of unusual.*
Americans often pronounce it as *kinda*.

C 4.03 **LISTENING SKILL—Listen for specific information** **Listen again and choose the correct option.**

1 Audrey often starts work …
 a at 6:00. **b** at 8:00. **c** at 10:00.
2 She frequently finishes work at …
 a six o'clock in the evening. **b** seven thirty in the evening. **c** eight or nine at night.
3 On weekends, Audrey almost always …
 a works. **b** spends time with her family. **c** goes to San Francisco.
4 Audrey and her family go to San Francisco to …
 a see her parents. **b** go to the zoo. **c** work.
5 Audrey thinks that her life is …
 a exciting. **b** normal. **c** boring.

D **IN PAIRS THINKING SKILL—Summarize** **Describe Audrey's life.**

A: She's married / an actress.
B: She has children / an interesting life / a difficult job.
A: She works from … to …
B: On weekdays / weekends / Saturdays / Sundays, she …
A: She doesn't often …

VOCABULARY frequency and time expressions

A **Complete the table with the words in the box.**

3:00	day	March 20	night	three times
a day	Friday	month	once	Tuesdays
a week	March	morning	the evening	twice
week	year	~~2020~~		

in	on	at	every	several times	… a day / month / year
2020					

B IN PAIRS Ask and answer questions. Use frequency expressions.

1 How often do you eat at restaurants?
2 How often does your family go on vacation?
3 How often do you play video games?
4 How often do you have English class?
5 How often do you go shopping?

GRAMMAR frequency adverbs

A Look at the scale. Then complete the rules.

100%	75%	50%	25%	10%	0%
always	usually	often	sometimes	rarely	never

I'm always tired!
We usually work a lot of hours.
Sometimes we go to San Francisco to see my parents.
I rarely work on Saturdays.

1 Frequency adverbs come **before** / **after** the verb *be*.
2 Frequency adverbs come **before** / **after** other verbs.
3 Frequency or time expressions come **at the end** / **at the beginning or end** of a sentence.

For more practice, go to page 147.

B Look at the scale. Then complete the sentences.

100%	75%	50%	25%	10%	0%
eats breakfast	sees friends on the weekend	listens to podcasts	talks on the phone	is sad	is late to work

1 Robert ____________ talks on the phone. (25%)
2 He ______________________________
3 ______________________________
4 ______________________________
5 ______________________________
6 ______________________________

SPEAKING

A Complete the survey for you.

How often do you …	You				
go out to eat?					
go to a movie?					
take a vacation?					
use social media?					

B IN GROUPS Write each group member's name at the top of the table in A. Ask and answer the questions for each group member. Use the Confident Communicator box to help you. Then discuss. Do the people in your group have similar routines or very different routines?

CONFIDENT COMMUNICATOR
KEEP TALKING

When you don't know the exact frequency of an activity, use words like *about*, *around*, and *more or less: about once a month, around four times a year, more or less twice a day.*

The Perfect Day

VOCABULARY routine activities

A Match the expressions from the box to the photos.

cook	do housework	get dressed	go to the gym
go out with friends	hang out at home	take a nap	take a shower

1  ____________

2  ____________

3  ____________

4  ____________

5  ____________

6  ____________

7  ____________

8  ____________

B IN PAIRS Discuss the activities using frequency expressions.

A: I often do housework.
B: I never take a nap.
A: I rarely cook.
B: I usually go to the gym in the morning.

LISTENING

a 

b 

A Look at the pictures. Which type of day off do you prefer?

B 4.04 LISTENING SKILL—Listen for gist Listen to a radio show. Write *C* (*crazy*) or *L* (*lazy*) for each caller.

1 Brendon: ____________
2 Carla: ____________
3 Ali: ____________
4 Melissa: ____________

C 4.04 IN PAIRS THINKING SKILL—Recall Listen again. List the activities each caller does on a day off.

1 Brendon: gets up late, ____________
2 Carla: takes a shower, ____________
3 Ali: goes to the gym, ____________
4 Melissa: hangs out at home, ____________

D IN PAIRS Compare your lists with another partner.

MAKE IT YOURS

Make a list of activities that you like doing on a day off.

WRITING

A **Read the blog post. In your opinion, is Olivia's day crazy or lazy? Discuss.**

THE PERFECT DAY OFF

March 2 3:32 p.m.

I love to write this blog, but I also love to have a day off! On my perfect day off, I usually get up late. I take a shower and get dressed. I go out and eat a big breakfast. After breakfast, I go for a walk. Then, I usually hang out with friends. We go to a café or go shopping. Sometimes we go to a movie. In the evening, I almost always order food, usually pizza. I don't like cooking! I never read blogs or use social media on my day off.

follow

B **Complete the table for you.**

	Activities on a Day Off
always	
usually	
often	
sometimes	
rarely	
never	

C **Write a paragraph about your perfect day off in your notebook.**

D IN PAIRS **Read your partner's paragraph. Answer the questions and make recommendations. Use your partner's comments to make any changes to your paragraph.**

1 Does your partner …

- **a** capitalize words correctly? Yes / No
- **b** use *be* correctly? Yes / No
- **c** have any spelling errors? Yes / No
- **d** have any grammar errors? Yes / No

SPEAKING

A IN GROUPS **Discuss your perfect day off. As you listen to each person, write *C* (*crazy*) or *L* (*lazy*), depending on the person's favorite type of day off.**

B **Take a class survey to see how many people enjoy lazy days and how many enjoy crazy days. Use the Confident Communicator box to help you.**

CONFIDENT COMMUNICATOR
KEEP TALKING

You can use negative verbs with *always*, *usually*, *often*, and *sometimes*. Notice the word order:

*I **don't always** eat breakfast.*
*I **don't usually** exercise on Saturdays.*
*I **don't often** get up late.*
*I **sometimes don't** check my email.*

Language and Life

Adaptability – An Interesting Life

A 4.05 **Read the social media web page. In your opinion, why is Andy bored? Discuss. Do your classmates agree?**

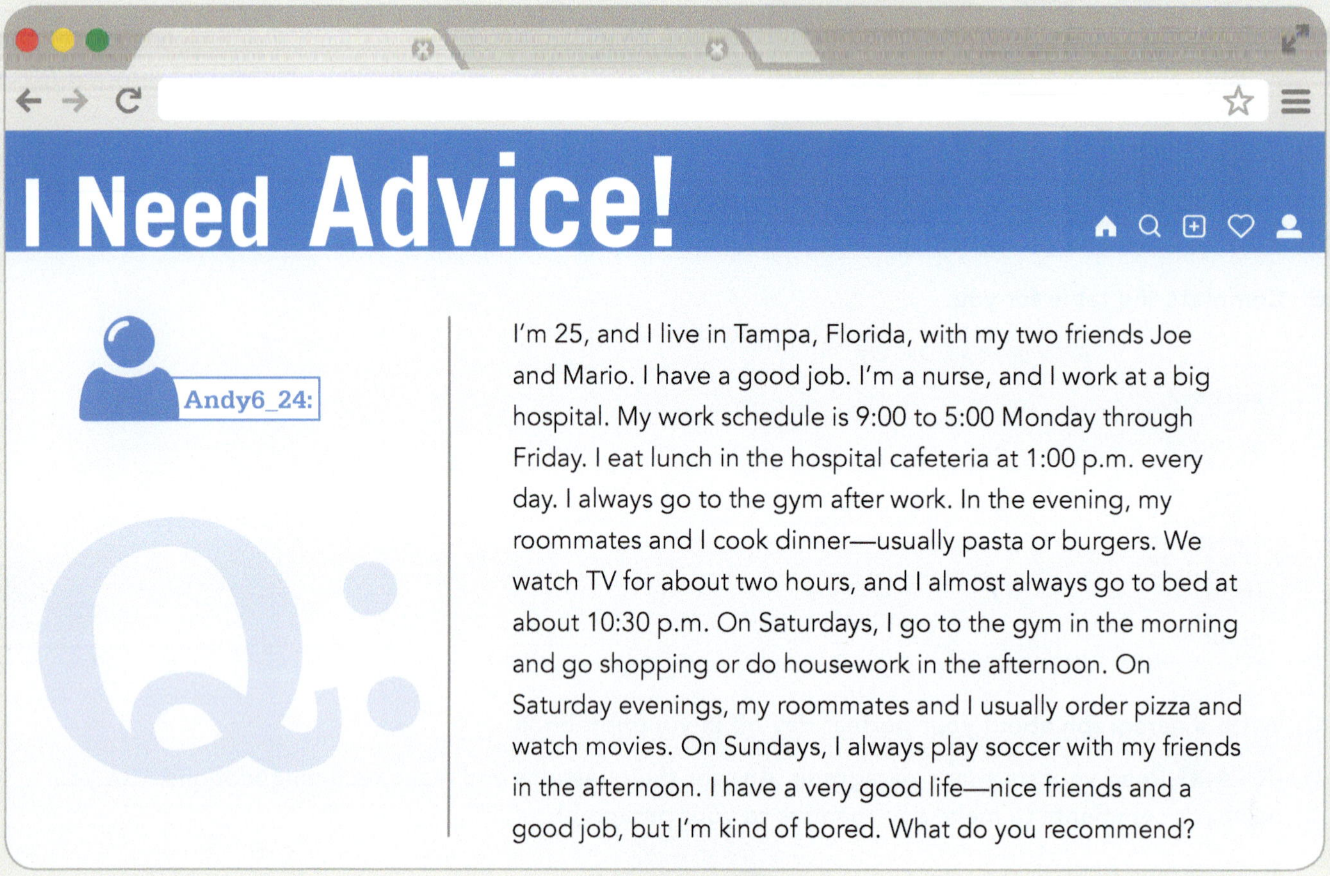

I'm 25, and I live in Tampa, Florida, with my two friends Joe and Mario. I have a good job. I'm a nurse, and I work at a big hospital. My work schedule is 9:00 to 5:00 Monday through Friday. I eat lunch in the hospital cafeteria at 1:00 p.m. every day. I always go to the gym after work. In the evening, my roommates and I cook dinner—usually pasta or burgers. We watch TV for about two hours, and I almost always go to bed at about 10:30 p.m. On Saturdays, I go to the gym in the morning and go shopping or do housework in the afternoon. On Saturday evenings, my roommates and I usually order pizza and watch movies. On Sundays, I always play soccer with my friends in the afternoon. I have a very good life—nice friends and a good job, but I'm kind of bored. What do you recommend?

B Complete the notes with information from the web page.

Weekdays:

9:00–5:00 *works at the hospital*
1:00 p.m.
after work
in the evening

Saturdays:
in the morning
in the afternoon
in the evening

Sundays:
in the afternoon

C **IN PAIRS** Write recommendations to Andy for making his life more interesting.

I Need Advice!

Hi, Andy. We have some suggestions. Don't always watch TV after dinner. Go out and ... Don't ... every day.

D **IN GROUPS** Think of more recommendations for Andy to make his life more interesting.

E **IN GROUPS** Discuss your routine. Give each other recommendations to make your lives more exciting.

MAKE IT DIGITAL

Post ideas for people to make their lives more interesting on your own social media site.

VOCABULARY review

SCORE: / 10

A Complete the sentences with verbs from the box.

exercise	go	get	get up	hang out
have	order	start	take	walk

I'm a dessert blogger, and I have a usual daily routine. I **1** ____________ at 9:00, **2** ____________ coffee, and **3** ____________ the dog. Then, I **4** ____________ a shower and **5** ____________ ready for my workday. I **6** ____________ work at 11:30. I eat lunch at a different restaurant every day. After lunch, I **7** ____________ a dessert from the menu to eat. In the afternoon, I write my blog. Sunday is my day off. I don't just **8** ____________ at home. After all those desserts, I **9** ____________ to the gym and **10** ____________ for an hour!

GRAMMAR review

SCORE: / 10

A Write the question that asks about the underlined information.

1 I talk to my friends several times a day. ____________
2 We do housework on Sundays. ____________
3 My sister works in a café on weekends. ____________
4 I eat cake every afternoon. ____________
5 He studies English because it's fun! ____________

B Rewrite the sentences with the words in parentheses.

1 Meg takes a nap in the afternoon. (often) ____________
2 Mr. Nelson is late for class. (never) ____________
3 Kyle sees his parents. (twice a year) ____________
4 Anita takes the train to work. (rarely) ____________
5 We're at the gym on Sundays. (always) ____________

16–20 correct: You can talk about daily activities and frequency. You can use simple present information questions and frequency adverbs.
0–15 correct: Look again at the Vocabulary and Grammar sections in the unit.

TOTAL SCORE: / 20

WHAT DO YOU KNOW NOW? Look back at page 37 and add the words you know now to the boxes.

FOLLOW A PRO — EMERGENCY SERVICES

Take the quiz about emergency services. Go to **Follow A Pro** on page 130 to find the answers. Then learn more about the emergency services industry.

1 The oldest emergency telephone number is 999. How old is it?
a over 70 years old **b** over 80 years old **c** over 90 years old

2 How many hours of training do you need to become a paramedic?
a about 2,000 **b** about 1,000 **c** about 500

3 What US state has a festival every year to celebrate its emergency workers?
a Washington **b** California **c** Alabama

4 70% of emergency medical technicians in the US are male.
a true **b** false

UNIT 5 Finding Your Way

WHAT DO YOU ALREADY KNOW?

1 **Think of places you usually go and places you sometimes go. Write the names of the places.**

2 **IN PAIRS Share and compare your information. Add more words to your list.**

Places I usually go

school

Places I sometimes go

museum

DISCUSS & SHARE

VIDEO

3 **IN GROUPS Watch the video and answer the question.**

SYM Do you ask for directions or try to find your way?

In this unit, you will ...

- talk about places to live, your neighborhood, and directions.
- use thinking skills: apply, evaluate, and analyze.
- read about unusual places to live.
- use strategies to keep talking by making guesses.
- use problem-solving skills to create a guide to your neighborhood.
- learn research skills for school and work.

Where Do You Live?

READING

A **Look at the pictures in B and discuss the questions. Do you want to live somewhere like this? Why or why not?**

B **5.01 READING SKILL—Scan for specific information** **Read the article and answer the questions.**

PLACES WE LIVE

For many young people, the idea of buying a **home** is important. But what happens when you don't have a lot of money to buy? Here are two interesting options for millennials.

Oscar Knight lives in a new apartment in an exciting **neighborhood** in London. "This is an **apartment building** designed for young people between the ages of 20 and 35," he says. "We live, work, and play all in one space. It's not boring at all! There are different spaces for us to use, such as a library, a community **garden**, a gym, an office, a popular restaurant, and a grocery store."

"London is expensive," says Layla, one of Oscar's neighbors. "But it's a fun **city**. I pay £330 per week here, but that includes Wi-Fi, electricity, water, and a gym. I never feel bored here. It's a great place to live, and the people are very friendly."

Eco-pod similar to Jay's eco-pod.

Jay Nilsson, from Sweden, lives in an unusual house. He has a one-room eco-pod. "This eco-pod is great," says Jay. "You can live wherever you want. My eco-pod is in my parents' **yard** on a quiet **street**, but I can move my eco-pod, too." Eco-pods are not cheap—Jay's eco-pod cost him almost $93,000. They are also very small—only 8 meters long. But there is a bed, a bathroom, and a tiny kitchen. It's good for one person only!

1 What city does Oscar live in? ___________
2 Does Layla think it is a good place for young people to live? ___________
3 Where does Jay live? ___________
4 How big is Jay's eco-pod? ___________

C **IN PAIRS THINKING SKILL—Apply** **Discuss your preferences and explain. Do you want to live in an apartment building like Oscar or in an eco-pod like Jay?**

VOCABULARY

A **Complete the definitions with words from the article.**

1 a place to live: h___________, a___________
2 an area around a house: g___________, y___________
3 the area around where you live: n___________
4 the people who live near you: n___________
5 a very large town: c___________
6 a road: s___________

MAKE IT YOURS

Find more words that describe your neighborhood and the house, apartment, or street where you live.

GRAMMAR adjectives

A **Circle adjectives in READING B.**

B **Read the grammar rules. Complete the examples from READING B.**

1 Use adjectives to describe nouns. Adjectives often come before a noun. Write three examples from the text.
a new apartment, ______________, ______________, ______________

2 Adjectives can also come after the verbs *be*, *look*, or *feel*. Write one example from the text.
London is expensive. ______________

3 Some adjectives end in *–ing* and describe things or places. Write one example from the text.
an exciting neighborhood, ______________

4 Some adjectives end in *–ed* and describe feelings. Write one example from the text.
excited, ______________

For more practice, go to page 148.

C **Unscramble and write the sentences.**

1 expensive / this / café / an / is / .
____

2 this / the / great / restaurant / at / popular / is / food / .
____

3 neighbors / very / noisy / my / are / .
____

4 class / boring / really / is / this / a / .
____

D **IN PAIRS Discuss your neighborhoods using adjectives.**

A: What's your neighborhood like? *B: It's quiet. How about yours?*

PRONUNCIATION syllable stress in multi-syllable adjectives

A **5.02 Say the words. Underline the stressed syllable. Then listen and check.**

1	lively	quiet	busy
2	expensive	exciting	important

B **5.03 Listen and notice how the stressed syllable is louder and longer than the unstressed syllables. Practice stressing the syllables.**

1 expensive houses 2 an exciting city 3 busy neighborhood

SPEAKING

A **Write two sentences that are true and one sentence that is not true about your home and neighborhood.**

B **IN GROUPS Read your sentences aloud. Ask your group members to guess which sentence is not true. Use the Confident Communicator box to help you.**

CONFIDENT COMMUNICATOR
KEEP TALKING

When you're not sure about something, you can make guesses:
It's just a guess, but …
It's difficult to say, but …
I bet it's …

LESSON 2 What's in Your Neighborhood?

VOCABULARY places in a neighborhood

A Write the places under the pictures with words from the box. Compare your answers with a partner.

apartment building	bus stop	coffee shop	grocery store
gym	high school	library	train station

1 
______

2 
______

3 
______

4 
______

5 
______

6 
______

7 
______

8 
______

B Use words from A to complete the table.

Places to ...

live/study	exercise	shop	travel to/from	hang out

MAKE IT REAL

Sometimes you hear different words for the same places in a neighborhood.

gym = fitness center, health club | *coffee shop = café*

grocery store = supermarket | *apartment (American English) = flat (British English)*

LISTENING

A Look at the pictures. Would you like to live in these neighborhoods?

B 5.04 LISTENING SKILL—Listen for specific information **Listen to the radio show. Check (✓) the places Elsa and Ahmed mention.**

	coffee shop	park	gym	bus stop	train station	grocery store	library	apartment building	high school
Elsa									
Ahmed									

C 5.04 **Listen again. Who likes their neighborhood? Discuss.**

D IN PAIRS THINKING SKILL—Evaluate **Compare and discuss where you want to live.**

1 What are the differences between living outside of a town or city and living close to the city?
2 Where do you like to live?

GRAMMAR *there is / there are*

A **Read the sentences. Complete the rules.**

There is a grocery store and a park.
There's no gym and no library.
Are there things to do or places to hang out in your neighborhood?
There's a coffee shop where I hang out with my friends.

1 We use *There is* and *There are* to talk about **things that exist** / **things that don't exist.**
2 We use *There is no* and *There are no* to talk about **things that exist** / **things that don't exist.**
3 *Are there …?* is the question form for **one thing** / **more than one thing.**
4 *There's* is the contraction of ***there is*** / ***there are.***

For more practice, go to page 148.

B **Find one mistake and write the correct sentences.**

1 There aren't a train station near my house. ____________________
2 Are there a gym in your neighborhood? ____________________
3 In my town, there a grocery store, but no library. ____________________
4 There's not coffee shop in my neighborhood. ____________________
5 There are a good restaurant near the bus stop. ____________________

C **Make notes about your neighborhood and what amenities you think it needs. Share with a partner.**

D **As a class, discuss your neighborhoods.**

SPEAKING

A **Draw a map of a neighborhood with at least six places on it in your notebook.**

B IN PAIRS **Discuss your maps. Use the Confident Communicator box to help you.**

Do not look at your partner's map. When your partner asks about a place on your map, put a check (✓). When your partner asks about all the places on your map, say *Bingo!* The first pair to find all the places on both maps wins.

A: Is there a library? *B: No, there's no library. / Yes, there's a library.*

CONFIDENT COMMUNICATOR
KEEP TALKING

Visitors often need information about a place from a person who knows the area. To say you know or don't know an area, say:

I'm from (near) here. *I'm (not) a local.*
I'm (not) from around here. *I (don't) live close by.*

VOCABULARY directions

A Match the directions to the pictures. Write the letters.

1 Take the first left. ____
2 Turn around. ____
3 Take the second left. ____
4 Go straight ahead. ____

B Look at the map. Write the answer.

1 It's next to the apartment building. ________
2 It's between the apartment building and the gym. ________
3 It's across from the grocery store. ________
4 It's on the corner of River Street and Third Avenue. ________

C Look at the map in B again. Then complete the directions.

1 A: Excuse me. How do I get to the high school? B: Go over the bridge. Then take the first ________.
2 A: Can you tell me how to get to the train station? B: Yes. Go ________ and then take the second right.
3 A: Is there a bus stop near here? B: It's over there, across from the ________.
4 A: How do I get to the library? B: Take the next ________. Then take another right.
5 A: Hi. Do you know where the coffee shop is? B: Yes. It's ________ the apartment building and the gym.

D IN PAIRS Discuss directions. Ask for and give directions to and from the places.

1 from the library to the bus stop
2 from the train station to the coffee shop
3 from the apartment building to the high school
4 from the park to the library

LISTENING

A IN PAIRS Check (✓) what you do if you get lost.

- ☐ call a friend or relative
- ☐ ask a person on the street for help
- ☐ keep walking or driving
- ☐ use a map on your phone

B 5.05 LISTENING SKILL—Listen for key words Listen to the conversations. Write the places the speakers want to go to.

1 Conversation 1: ______________
2 Conversation 2: ______________
3 Conversation 3: ______________
4 Conversation 4: ______________
5 Conversation 5: ______________

C 5.05 Listen again and write the directions in your notebook.

D IN PAIRS THINKING SKILL—Analyze Discuss.

1 Where do you sometimes get lost?
2 What do you do?
3 Do you ask for help? Who do you ask?
4 How often do you get lost?

WRITING

A Read the instant messages. Does Samantha know how to get to the coffee shop? Discuss.

B Match the words from the box to the abbreviations.

Samantha:
Hi! How RU? Meet for coffee tomorrow?

Melissa:
Sure. Baker's? 4 p.m.?

Samantha:
OK. Send directions!

Melissa:
Main St. to 3 Ave. Cross the bridge. Turn left at Harry's. Take next right. Baker's bldg is on the corner. CU 2morrow!

building	tomorrow	are you
see you	avenue	street

1 Ave ______________
2 2morrow ______________
3 CU ______________
4 RU ______________
5 bldg ______________
6 St ______________

C Rewrite the instant messages in complete sentences in your notebook. Don't use abbreviations.

D IN PAIRS Practice writing directions. Text or write directions to your partner using abbreviations and/or emojis. Then write your partner's directions in complete sentences.

SPEAKING

A IN PAIRS Practice the conversation. Use the Confident Communicator box to help you.

A: Excuse me. Where is the bus stop?
B: It's straight ahead. Go one more block.

B IN PAIRS Role-play asking for and giving directions. Then change roles and role-play again.

Student A: You are lost. Ask how to get to places from your school.
Student B: Give directions to Student A.

CONFIDENT COMMUNICATOR
START TALKING

To ask for directions, say:
Excuse me. Where is/are …?
How do I get to …?
Can you tell me where the … is/are?
Is there a/an … nearby?

Language and Life

Problem-solving – A Neighborhood Guide

A 5.06 **Read the magazine article. Is Katy happy in her new neighborhood? Discuss.**

A New Place to Call Home

Name: Katy Morgan
From: Austin, Texas

I'm Katy. I'm from the United States, but now I live in a small neighborhood outside Cusco, Peru. Cusco is an amazing city. Machu Picchu is very close by. I have my own business here. I organize eco-tours around the area.

Life in Peru is great. I speak Spanish, so communication isn't a problem. There are other differences. In the States, things happen fast and people run from place to place. Here, life is slow, and I like it that way!

My neighborhood is small, but there are stores, restaurants (amazing food!), and a beautiful main square (the Plaza de Armas) in the city center. I live in a one-bedroom apartment on a quiet street. There's a small coffee shop across from my house, so I hang out with my neighbors before work. People here like to get together and talk.

It's hard to find a place to live when you arrive in a new city. There's a great company called Home Abroad Rentals. They find apartments for people from other countries who are new to Cusco. They match people to the right home. I'm happy Cusco is the place I call home.

B **Read the profiles of people who want to find a place to live in your city. Make notes about neighborhoods that are good for each person, and say why those places are good.**

Profile 1

Name: James Quigley

Age: 28

From: Johannesburg, South Africa

Job: translator for a large tech company

Prefers: to live outside the town/city center; to live alone

Wants to find: a small house with a yard

Hobbies: swimming, cooking, going out to eat, seeing friends, biking

follow

Profile 2

Name: Christine Summers

Age: 23

From: Sydney, Australia

Job: English teacher

Prefers: to live in the town/city center; to have roommates

Wants to find: a one-bedroom apartment; a shared house

Hobbies: dancing, running, reading, traveling

follow

C **IN PAIRS** **Compare your ideas for the profiles.**

A: I think a good neighborhood for Christine is … because there's a park.

B: I think … is a good neighborhood for James because there are houses with yards.

D **IN PAIRS** **Complete a neighborhood guide for an area you know well.**

Neighborhood guide for: ______________________

Types of housing available: ______________________

Sports facilities: ______________________

Popular restaurants: ______________________

Good places to shop: ______________________

How to get around (bus/train): ______________________

Directions from housing to one or two other interesting places: ______________________

____

____

E **IN GROUPS** **Discuss your guides. Then share with the class.**

MAKE IT DIGITAL

Go online and look for more information about the neighborhood. Include any information you think is useful.

VOCABULARY review

SCORE: / 10

A Complete the sentences with words from the box.

across	boring	expensive	on	square
apartment	difficult	gym	popular	tiny

Jasper: I live near the university. There are many students here, so it's not an expensive part of town. I live in an old **1** ________ with only one room. It's **2** ________ , but it's OK for me.

Kate: I live with my parents. It's a big house near the main **3** ________ in town, but there is nothing fun to do in the neighborhood. It's **4** ________ .

Ed: I have a new apartment **5** ________ the corner of Main and First. I like it, but I pay a lot—about $1,300 a month. It's a very **6** ________ neighborhood.

Kim: I love my neighborhood. There are fun coffee shops, great restaurants, and a new **7** ________ to work out in. The neighborhood is **8** ________ with students and families.

Neil: My new house is on Third Street. From here, cross the bridge and then turn left. It's **9** ________ from the park. It's not **10** ________ to find.

GRAMMAR review

SCORE: / 10

A Combine the two sentences into one.

1 Cusco is a city. Cusco is exciting.

____

2 It's a place. It's friendly.

____

3 There are many neighborhoods. They're lively.

____

4 There's a market. It's very interesting.

____

5 Cusco has some buildings. They're very old.

____

B Match the sentence beginning (1–5) to the sentence end (a–e). Write the letter.

1 There are ____
2 There is ____
3 There's no ____
4 Is there ____
5 Are there ____

a many Cuban restaurants?
b an airport near the city?
c people from all over the world.
d train to Everglades National Park.
e a zoo with lots of different animals.

16–20 correct: You can talk about places in a neighborhood and give directions. You can use adjectives and *there is*/*there are*.
0–15 correct: Look again at the Vocabulary and Grammar sections in the unit.

TOTAL SCORE: / 20

WHAT DO YOU KNOW NOW? Look back at page 47 and add the words you know now to the boxes.

STUDY SKILLS RESEARCH SKILLS

Take the quiz about research skills. Go to **Study Skills** on page 131 to find the answers. Then learn more about research skills.

1 About ... people around the world work full-time as researchers.
a 5.3 million b 7.8 million c 10 million

2 It takes the average person ... to read one page.
a one minute b two minutes c three minutes

3 Only 12% of teachers say their students use books for research.
a true b false

4 About 95% of internet users believe that most or all of the information they find online is true.
a true b false

UNIT 6 Going Viral

WHAT DO YOU ALREADY KNOW?

1 **Think of words about social media and the internet. Write the words or draw the icons of apps you use.**

2 **IN PAIRS** **Share and compare your information. Add more words to your lists.**

Social media

Internet

DISCUSS & SHARE

VIDEO

3 **IN GROUPS** **Watch the video and answer the question.**

SYM How much time do you spend online?

In this unit, you will …

- talk about media use, computer equipment, and online business.
- use thinking skills: analyze and evaluate.
- read about social media use and employment.
- use strategies to keep talking by showing interest and asking follow-up questions.
- use critical thinking skills to analyze the pros and cons of a digital detox.
- follow a social media marketing manager to learn about this job and the skills needed for this industry.

You and Social Media

READING

A IN PAIRS **Discuss the social media apps you use and how often you use them.**

A: I use … every day. *B: I never use …*

B 6.01 READING SKILL—Predict information **Read the article and guess the missing information. Then check your answers below.**

Social Media Use and Employment

Do some things about social media make you **angry**?
If your answer is "yes," read on …

Young adults are spending a lot of time on social media these days. According to Statista, about **1** ______________ billion people use social media. Are you **surprised**? That's about one-third of the world's population! In the US, around **2** ______________% of people aged 16 to 24 have social media accounts. On average, they spend **3** ______________ minutes per day—almost two hours—on social media. **4** ______________ has more social media users than any other country—596 million. That number is growing all the time.

Many people are **afraid** that employers are getting information about them from social media. This information can make them feel **embarrassed**.

A study by Statista from 2017 shows that **5** ______________% of employers look at social media profiles before they hire someone. So, be very careful and check your settings. Keep your social media profiles for family and friends only.

Read more

Answer Key for Reading B:
1 2.5; **2** 98; **3** 109; **4** China; **5** 61

VOCABULARY

A Read the sentences (1–4) and match the words in bold to the emojis (a–d). Write the letter.

1 2.5 billion people use social media! Really? I'm **surprised**! ______
2 I'm **embarrassed** when I tell people I don't use social media. ______
3 I'm **mad** when there are ads on social media sites all the time. ______
4 Don't be **afraid** to take a break from social media. ______

a 
b 
c 
d 

B THINKING SKILL—Analyze **Which of these opinions do you agree with? Why?**

1 Social media friends are not real friends.
2 Social media is a great way to share information.

MAKE IT YOURS

Which emojis do you use most often? Send an emoji to a classmate to say how you are feeling. Ask that person to say in English how you are feeling.

GRAMMAR present progressive

A Read the examples. Then choose the correct option to complete the rules.

Young adults are spending a lot of time on social media these days.
Employers are now using social media sites.
They're getting information about future employees.

1 Use the present progressive for things that are happening **every day** / **now**.
2 Form the present progressive with the verb *be* + **–ing** / **infinitive**.
3 When a verb ends in –e, remove –*e* and add –*ing*: *use* becomes *using*, *take* becomes ***takeing*** / ***taking***.
4 When a verb ends in a vowel + consonant, double the last consonant and add –*ing*: *get* becomes *getting*, *stop* becomes ***stopping*** / ***stoping***.
5 When a verb ends in –*ie*, change the –*ie* to –*y* and add –*ing*: *lie* becomes *lying*, *tie* becomes ***tying*** / ***tieing***.

For more practice, go to page 149.

B Complete the conversation with the present progressive.

Jenny: Hi, Gemma. **1** What ____________ you ____________ (do)?
Gemma: **2** Oh, I ____________ (look) at things online.
Jenny: **3** Why____________ you ____________? (not study)
Gemma: **4** I ____________ (take) a break. So what's up?
Jenny: **5** I ____________ (call) because I need help.
Gemma: Are you worried about the exam tomorrow?
Jenny: **6** No, I ____________ (buy) some new shoes online. Can you look at them?
Gemma: Sure!

C IN PAIRS Role-play a phone conversation. Talk about what you are doing now and how you are feeling.

SPEAKING

A Complete the table with the things you are usually doing at these times and days.

	Tuesday	Friday	Saturday
7 a.m.			
12 p.m.			
6 p.m.			
11 p.m.			

B IN PAIRS Ask and answer questions about what you are doing at these times. Use the Confident Communicator box to help you.

A: It's 7 a.m. on Sunday. What are you doing? *B: I'm sleeping.*
A: And how are you feeling? *B: I'm relaxed!*

CONFIDENT COMMUNICATOR
START TALKING

To ask about feelings, say: *Are you OK? Is everything all right? What's the matter?*
To describe how you are feeling, say: *I'm feeling … today. / I'm sad about … / I'm happy about … / I'm tired / I'm sleepy / I'm hungry.*

LESSON 2 **Vlogging**

VOCABULARY technology equipment

A Match the words from the box to the pictures.

microphone	headphones	keyboard	screen
smartphone	mouse	tablet	webcam

1 
____

2 
____

3 
____

4 
____

5 
____

6 
____

7 
____

8 
____

B Complete the information about vlogging with the words in the box.

microphone smartphone tablets webcam

So, you want to be a vlogger?

Here are some of the things you need.

To film your vlog, you need a video camera. If you are sitting at home with your computer, you can use the **1** ________________. Some vloggers use the camera on their **2** ________________ to make videos. The screens are very small, but they work fine. **3** ________________ are also OK to use, but a computer makes your vlog look more professional. When you speak, you use a **4** ________________. People need to hear what you are saying, so get a good one.

Happy vlogging!

MAKE IT YOURS

Compound words are two different words put together.
desk + *top* = ***desk**top*
web + *camera* = ***web**cam*
What other compound words do you know?

LISTENING

A IN PAIRS Match vlog types from the box to the pictures.

computer gaming food product reviews travel

1 
____

2 
____

3 
____

4 
____

B 6.02 **Listen to the vloggers and match them to the vlog types in A.**

1 Speaker 1: ____________
2 Speaker 2: ____________
3 Speaker 3: ____________
4 Speaker 4: ____________

C 6.03 LISTENING SKILL—Listen for fact and opinion **Listen and choose *Fact* or *Opinion*.**

1 Fact / Opinion
2 Fact / Opinion
3 Fact / Opinion
4 Fact / Opinion
5 Fact / Opinion

D THINKING SKILL—Evaluate **Discuss the statement. Do you agree? What do you think makes a good vlogger?**

A good vlogger is like the boy or girl next door—someone who feels like I do about things.

GRAMMAR present progressive vs. simple present

A Read the sentences. Underline the present progressive verbs. Circle the simple present verbs.

1 Right now, I'm using my laptop to upload videos …
2 I spend about six months of the year away from home …
3 I'm studying to be a computer programmer.
4 People always ask me for advice …

B Choose the correct option to complete the rules.

1 We use the simple present to talk about things that happen regularly / now or around now.
2 We use the present progressive to talk about things that are happening regularly / now or around now.

For more practice, go to page 150.

C Choose the correct option. Is the question in simple present or present progressive?

1 Where is your laptop?
a simple present **b** present progressive
2 What are you watching on your laptop?
a simple present **b** present progressive
3 What kind of camera do you use to make vlogs?
a simple present **b** present progressive
4 What famous vloggers are you following?
a simple present **b** present progressive

D IN PAIRS **Ask and answer the questions from C.**

SPEAKING

A Write complete questions in your notebook with the words given.

1 What / do / do?
2 What / do / generally / vlog / about?
3 How / usually / make / your vlog?
4 How / often / vlog?

B IN PAIRS **Role-play. Use the Confident Communicator box to help you.**

Student A: Imagine you are a well-known music vlogger.
Student B: Imagine you are a famous skateboarding vlogger. Ask and answer questions in A to find out more about your partner.

C IN GROUPS **Discuss which vlogs you watch. Do you have your own vlog?**

CONFIDENT COMMUNICATOR
KEEP TALKING

It's important to show interest when someone is talking to you:
Oh, right. *I see.* *Uh-huh.* *Really?*
When things are very interesting, your voice is usually higher and louder:
No way! *Wow, that's amazing!* *You're kidding!*

LESSON 3 **Buying and Selling Online**

LISTENING

A Check (✓) the things you like to buy and sell in online stores.

☐ books
☐ clothes
☐ electronics (smartphones, headphones)
☐ music, movies, video games
☐ sports equipment (soccer balls, athletic shoes, baseball bats)
☐ other: ______________________

B 6.04 LISTENING SKILL—Listen for the main idea **Listen to an interview with an internet business owner. Then answer the question.**

1 What does he buy and sell? ______________

C 6.04 **Listen again and answer the questions.**

1 How old is Luca?
2 Where does he buy and sell things?
3 How much money does he make per item?
4 How often does Luca add new pictures to his website?
5 What is his day job?

D THINKING SKILL—Evaluate **Consider some of the differences between shopping online and shopping in a store. What do you prefer? Why?**

I like shopping in a store because I can see and touch what I'm buying.

VOCABULARY technology phrases

A 6.05 **Listen and complete the phrases with words from the box.**

go post send take update upload

1 ______________ a text message
2 ______________ pictures
3 ______________ comments
4 ______________ my profile
5 ______________ viral
6 ______________ a selfie

B Match the phrases from A (1–6) to the definitions (a–f). Write the number.

a take a picture of yourself on a smartphone _____
b write your opinion about something online _____
c communicate by typing on your smartphone _____
d become very popular on the internet _____
e copy a picture to the internet _____
f put new information about yourself on a social media site _____

PRONUNCIATION /ŋ/

A 6.06 **Listen and notice the /ŋ/ sound for the letters *–ng*.**

1 kin king
2 sin sing
3 thin thing

B 6.07 IN PAIRS **Listen and practice saying the sentences. Is your partner using the /ŋ/ sound correctly?**

1 Sing this song.
2 The teacher is talking.
3 I'm listening to music.

WRITING

A Check (✓) the details to include when you want to sell a product online.

☐ information about the product (name, type, color)
☐ what it does (takes pictures, plays music, etc.)
☐ where it is from
☐ condition (excellent, good, used, never used, etc.)
☐ why you're selling it
☐ the price

B Read and compare the two social media ads. Then discuss the questions.

1 Which ad do you like more?
2 Which ad makes you want to buy the headphones?

A

A pair of headphones for sale. They are good for listening to music. They are white. They are in good condition. They come from China. They cost $60. I am selling them for $45 because I want the money to buy new headphones.

follow

B

Hi! I'm selling my BodeA345 headphones. White. They're amazing! Fantastic sound. Very comfortable. Excellent condition. $40

follow

C Write *A* or *B*.

This ad …

1 uses positive adjectives. ______
2 doesn't use complete sentences. ______
3 doesn't use the same phrases for every sentence. ______
4 gives information that isn't important. ______

D Write a social media ad for something you want to sell online in your notebook.

SPEAKING

A Write sentences in your notebook about how you use technology and how often you do it.

I upload pictures to my social media profile about once a week.
I don't take selfies on my smartphone very often.

B IN GROUPS **Discuss your online activity and how you use technology. Use the Confident Communicator box to help you.**

CONFIDENT COMMUNICATOR
KEEP TALKING

To keep a conversation going, it's a good idea to ask for more information. When someone gives you a *yes/no* answer, you can ask follow-up questions. They usually begin with *How*, *Where*, *When*, *What*, and *Who*.
Do you take selfies?
How often do you take them?
What social media sites do you use?

Language and Life

Critical Thinking – A Digital Detox

A 6.08 **Read the article. Then answer the questions.**

Digital Detox

How to Do a Digital Detox

June 21 12:10

Are you spending too much time using your phone? Check the things that are true for you to find out:

- I check social media before I get out of bed. ☐
- I send messages while I have breakfast. ☐
- I often take my phone to the bathroom. ☐
- I never go out without my phone. ☐

Did you check three or four? Then, it may be time for a digital detox. Mandy Morgan, a social media expert, gives us this advice …

"This isn't about tech devices," she explains. "It's about understanding what is healthy. People usually feel good when they don't use their smartphones all the time."

Morgan says that a seven-day detox helps with your sleep, your studies, and how you feel. She asks people to check their screen time and count how many times a day they pick up their phone.

When you do a digital detox, you don't have your phone all the time. For seven days, you practice when and where you use your smartphone. You learn to leave your phone at home sometimes.

Marcia Estefan (DJ Blade), 23, is a club DJ from Brasilia. She is also studying to be a doctor. "I use my phone all the time," she explains. "I never think about how often I look at my screen." These days Marcia doesn't use her phone often. She rarely takes it out with her in the evening. "It makes me think about how I use technology and that's a good thing."

Before the Digital Detox
Screen Time Per Day: 3 hours 20 minutes
Picks Up Her Phone: 56 times a day

After the Digital Detox
Screen Time Per Day: 1 hour 50 minutes
Picks Up Her Phone: 23 times a day

Read more

1. Mandy Morgan says tech devices are bad for your health. Yes / No
2. You do a digital detox for one month. Yes / No
3. A digital detox can help you in different areas of your life. Yes / No
4. Marcia thinks that doing a digital detox is a good idea. Yes / No

B **IN PAIRS** **Discuss the questions.**

1 How much screen time do you have every day?
2 Do you think you use your phone too much? Be honest!

C **IN GROUPS** **Consider the pros (+) and cons (–) of doing a digital detox. Add other ideas of your own.**

Pros (+)
have time to think in class
have real conversations
your ideas: ______________________________

Cons (–)
the internet helps us study/learn
we know what our family/friends are doing
your ideas: ______________________________

D **Read the digital detox rules. As a class, decide if you want to have a digital detox for one class or one day.**

Digital detox rules

- Make your classroom a phone-free zone. No phones allowed!
- Put your phone in your pocket when you are talking or eating.
- Put your phone away on your way to/from school.
- Keep your phone on airplane mode in class, or leave it at home for a day.

E **Do the digital detox and make notes about how you feel.**

MAKE IT DIGITAL

Record a video on your smartphone about how you feel after a digital detox. Share your videos as a class. What did your classmates think?

VOCABULARY review

SCORE: / 10

A Choose the correct option.

1 Do you want to **play** / **go** / **take** a selfie with me?
2 I'm very **afraid** / **mad** / **embarrassed**. My new printer doesn't work.
3 Please **post** / **download** / **take** a comment after you read my blog.
4 I always use my smartphone to **play** / **send** / **do** a text message.
5 Please use my laptop to **create** / **play** / **go** an online profile.
6 It's easy to download an app with this **headphones** / **tablet** / **webcam**.
7 I sometimes use my desktop to **go** / **read** / **upload** a picture.
8 I'm **surprised** / **afraid** / **embarrassed**. She is giving away her new song.
9 I **be** / **use** / **update** my profile online once or twice a month.
10 Look into your **mouse** / **webcam** / **keyboard** to make a video.

GRAMMAR review

SCORE: / 10

A Complete the conversation with the correct simple present or present progressive form of the verb in parentheses.

Clare: Hey! What **1** ____________ you ____________ (do)?
Matt: Not much. I **2** ____________ (watch) a movie. You?
Clare: I **3** ____________ (study) at the library.
Matt: Again?
Clare: You know I usually **4** ____________ (come) here after class. Quick question: **5** ____________ you ____________ (use) headphones with your laptop?
Matt: Sure. I **6** ____________ (use) them right now.
Clare: What kind?
Matt: They're called AudioPlus. Electronics World **7** ____________ (sell) them.
Clare: Good to know. I need some. The people here are noisy! They **8** ____________ (talk) a lot. They **9** ____________ (not study)!
Matt: Well, get these. They always **10** ____________ (work) great!
Clare: Thanks! Gotta go—see you tomorrow.

16–20 correct: You can talk about emotions and technology. You can use the present progressive and simple present.
0–15 correct: Look again at the Vocabulary and Grammar sections in the unit.

TOTAL SCORE: / 20

WHAT DO YOU KNOW NOW? Look back at page 57 and add the words you know now to the box.

FOLLOW A PRO MARKETING

Take the quiz about marketing. Go to **Follow A Pro** on page 132 to find the answers. Then learn more about the marketing field.

1 In New York, around … people work in marketing full-time.
a 17,000 **b** 31,000 **c** 52,000

2 More customers go to a website when the company has a regular blog.
a true **b** false

3 How do 90% of businesses respond when customers complain?
a by social media **b** by email **c** by phone

4 When customers have a bad experience with a company, about 4% complain. What do the other 96% do?
a They buy the product again. **b** They tell their friends. **c** They never buy from that company again.

UNIT 7 Fit for Life

WHAT DO YOU ALREADY KNOW?

1 **Think of words you know about popular sports. Write a list of words for individual sports and team sports.**

2 **IN PAIRS** **Share and compare your information. Add more words to your lists.**

Individual sports

Team sports

DISCUSS & SHARE

VIDEO

3 **IN GROUPS** **Watch the video and answer the question.**

SYM Do you prefer individual or team sports?

In this unit, you will ...

- talk about the body, abilities, sports, and exercise.
- use thinking skills: analyze, decide, and evaluate.
- read about fitness gadgets.
- use strategies to start and keep talking by buying time and using your imagination.
- use decision-making skills to design an outdoor gym for your city.
- learn tips for effective group work.

VOCABULARY

A IN PAIRS **Look at the picture. Use words in the box to label the parts of the body.**

arm	back	foot	head	knee	leg	shoulder	neck

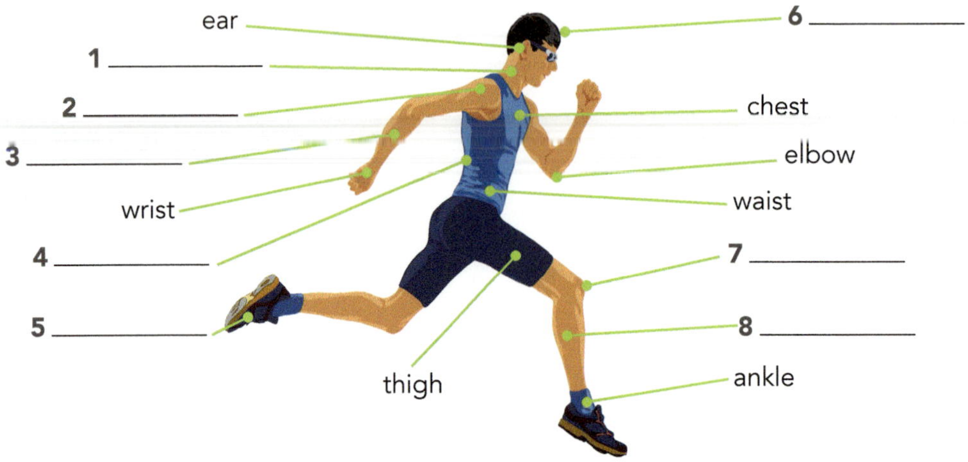

MAKE IT YOURS

Label any other parts of the body you know. Share your ideas in groups.

READING

A **Match the words in the box to the pictures (1–4).**

ankle sensor	fitness tracker	sports camera	underwater headphones

1 
____

2 
____

3 
____

4 
____

B 7.01 READING SKILL—Read for gist **Read the magazine article. Then complete with the gadget that matches the review.**

New GADGET Reviews

Are you looking for a new fitness gadget? Four athletes give their opinion about these gadgets.

1 ___________ Daniella, Boston. This is great. You can wear it on your **arm** or your **ankle**. It records your steps, your calories, and your sleep. You can use it when you ride a bike, run, walk, play volleyball, do judo, and every kind of sport. $76 ★★★★½

2 ___________ Miguel, Puebla. I love swimming and listening to music at the same time. I can swim really fast when I listen to music. These go around your **neck** and fit in your **ears**. They're very comfortable. $200 ★★★½

3 ___________ Felix, Sagres. It can take videos when I'm surfing. But when I'm on my surfboard, I can't hold it in my **hand**. I put it on my surfboard instead. You can also wear it on your **head** or on your **shoulder**. It takes pictures, too. $152 ★★★★

4 ___________ Clare, Santa Fe. You wear it on your **foot** and it checks that you're running correctly. Can you wash it? No, you can't wash it, even when it's dirty. It's expensive, in my opinion, but it's useful for professional runners. $120 ★★½

C THINKING SKILL—Analyze **Take a class survey. What gadgets do your classmates think are useful? Do you agree?**

GRAMMAR *can/can't* (ability)

A **Read the magazine article in READING B again. Underline the sentences with *can* and *can't*.**

B **Choose the correct option to complete the rules.**

1 Use *can/can't* to talk about …	**a** habits.	**b** abilities.
2 After *can/can't*, use a …	**a** verb.	**b** noun.
3 The contraction of *cannot* is …	**a** cant.	**b** can't.

For more practice, go to page 151.

C **Rewrite the sentences correctly.**

1 I can to play cricket. ____________________

2 She cans dance. ____________________

3 Can not you swim? ____________________

4 Yes, I can't. ____________________

5 He no can't play tennis. ____________________

D **IN PAIRS Ask and answer questions about the sports you can and can't do.**

PRONUNCIATION *can/can't*

A **7.02 Listen. Choose the words you hear.**

1 Can / Can't you swim?

2 I can / can't.

3 Can / Can't you come to a new water polo class with me?

4 Sorry, I can / can't. I play tennis then.

B **IN PAIRS Practice saying the conversation. Notice the /t/ sound in *can't*.**

SPEAKING

A **Check (✓) the things you can or can't do. Complete with your own ideas.**

	Can	Can't
1 play soccer	☐	☐
2 sing	☐	☐
3 cook Italian food	☐	☐
4 ____________	☐	☐
5 ____________	☐	☐

B **IN GROUPS Ask and answer questions about your abilities. Discuss information about what you like or dislike. Use the Confident Communicator box to help you.**

A: Can you surf? *B: Yes, I can, and I really enjoy it.*

CONFIDENT COMMUNICATOR
START TALKING

To ask about abilities and likes, use these phrases:

Can you …?

Yes, I can …, and I really enjoy it.

Yes, I can …, but I don't really like it.

No, I can't …, but I can … Can you …?

LESSON 2 Unusual Ball Games

VOCABULARY ball game action words

A IN PAIRS Match the verbs from the box to the pictures (1–8).

bounce	catch	hit	hold
kick	pass	throw	touch

1

____

2

____

3

____

4

____

5

____

6

____

7

____

8

____

B Choose the correct option.

1 Basketball players can **bounce** / **kick** the ball during the game.
2 In soccer, the players use their feet to **pass** / **hold** the ball.
3 Lacrosse players **hold** / **catch** the ball in a net.
4 Football players **throw** / **bounce** the ball between them.
5 You **kick** / **hit** the ball with a bat in baseball.
6 Tennis players usually **hold** / **kick** the ball in their left hand when they serve.

C IN PAIRS Think about popular ball games in your country. Talk about what the players can and can't do with the ball.

In basketball, players can bounce the ball. They can't kick the ball.

LISTENING

A Look at the pictures and think about the questions.

1 What do you know about these sports?
2 Do they look like other sports you know?

Bossaball

360ball

footgolf

B 7.03 LISTENING SKILL—Listen for the main idea **Listen and write the name of the ball games from A.**

1 David: ______________. **2** Claudia: ______________. **3** Marco: ______________.

C IN PAIRS THINKING SKILL—Deduce **Think about the three sports you learned about and discuss the question.**

Which game do you think people your age want to play?

MAKE IT REAL

When people talk about the sports they do regularly, they often leave out the verb *go*.
I hike. = *I go hiking.*
I swim. = *I go swimming.*

GRAMMAR adverbs of manner

A Read the examples. Then complete the rules.

I can throw the ball hard.
You have to play fast.
My friend plays it well.
You have to kick the ball gently.
I can kick it easily.

1 Use adverbs of manner to describe **an action** / **a thing**.
2 Adverbs of manner go **before** / **after** the main verb.
3 To form an adverb of manner, add ______________ to the adjective.
4 When a word ends in *–y*, add ______________.
5 Some irregular adverbs are the same word as the adjective: *fast–fast, hard–*______________.
6 One irregular adverb looks completely different from the adjective: *good–*______________.

For more practice, go to page 151.

B Choose the correct form of the adverb or adjective.

1 Please drive **careful** / **carefully**.
2 Fernando is a **slow** / **slowly** swimmer.
3 Todd is a fast runner. He runs **good** / **well**.
4 This is a library. Please speak **quiet** / **quietly**.
5 Patti speaks **angry** / **angrily** to me sometimes.

C IN PAIRS **Write activities from the unit in your notebook. Add adverbs to the things you can and can't do. Then ask and answer questions.**

A: I can't cook Italian food well. Can you? *B: No, I can't, but I can run fast.*

SPEAKING

A IN PAIRS **Make a list of famous athletes that you know and the sports that they play.**

B IN PAIRS **Play a game. Describe a famous athlete in one sentence. Your partner tries to guess who it is. Use the Confident Communicator box to help you.**

CONFIDENT COMMUNICATOR
START TALKING

Sometimes at the beginning of a conversation, you need time to organize your ideas. You can "buy time" by using these phrases:
Give me a minute to think about this …
Let me think about this for a second …

LESSON 3 **Exercising**

VOCABULARY exercise words

A Match the words from the box to the exercises (1–8).

bend lift pull push stand stretch turn twist

1 
____

2 
____

3 
____

4 
____

5 
____

6 
____

7 
____

8 
____

B 7.04 Listen and complete the text.

One of the exercises that I do at the gym is very hard. It's called *the deadlift with an overhead press.* You **1** _______________ with your feet on the floor. Then, you **2** _______________ the weight (I use a 10 kilogram) up to your chest. You **3** _______________ it there for about five seconds. Then, you **4** _______________ your knees and **5** _______________ the weight up above your head. It's not easy to **6** _______________ your arms so they're straight. I can usually only hold it above my head for about 10 seconds. I'm amazed how weightlifters do this all the time!

LISTENING

A As a class, answer the question.

1 What do you think the word *deskercise* means?

B 7.05 LISTENING SKILL—Listen for specific information Listen and choose the word you hear for each exercise.

1 Exercise 1: shoulder / back
2 Exercise 2: legs / arms
3 Exercise 3: head / hand
4 Exercise 4: back / neck
5 Exercise 5: knee / foot

C 7.05 Listen again and do the exercises. How do they make you feel?

D THINKING SKILL—Evaluate Take a class survey. What parts of the body do you need to stretch when you work at a desk all day?

MAKE IT REAL

To "hit the gym" is a phrase people use when they decide to go to the gym regularly.
I need to get some exercise. I'm going to hit the gym.

WRITING

A **Read the job ad. Which job are you interested in?**

Are you free to work on weekends and holidays?

We are looking for people who can speak English to work at Our International Spa. We offer good pay, plus the use of our gym.

The jobs available are:

- teaching an adult volleyball class
- working in the café
- teaching swimming
- working in the beauty salon
- working at our reception desk

Please email *k.smith@ourspa.co* by Friday, June 21. Be sure to send a list of your abilities.

B **Make a list of your abilities in your notebook. Then decide which jobs in the ad are right for you.**

C **Complete the email.**

New Message

From: ____________

To: k.smith@ourspa.co Cc Bcc

Subject: Employment at Our International Spa

Dear Sir/Madam,

I'm writing about a job at Our International Spa. I am ____________ years old and I live in ____________.

I'm interested in the job of ____________.

I think I am a good person for this job because ____

____.

I look forward to hearing from you.

Regards,

____________.

Send

SPEAKING

A IN PAIRS **Role-play a job interview. Use the Confident Communicator box to help you.**

Student A: You are K. Smith, the spa owner. Ask questions about why Student B wants the job.
Student B: Answer Student A's questions. Say why you are good for the job.

A: What job are you interested in? *B: I'm interested in … because …*

CONFIDENT COMMUNICATOR
KEEP TALKING

In speaking exercises in class, you don't need to say something that is true about yourself. The important thing is to say something. When you can't think of anything true to say, use your imagination.

Language and Life

Decision-making – Outdoor Gyms

A Look at the pictures and discuss the question as a class.

1 Where do you like to exercise?

B 7.06 Read the article. Then answer the questions below.

Outdoor Gyms Around the World

Many cities around the world have outdoor gyms. You see them on the beaches of Rio de Janeiro and in the parks in Shanghai or Spain. Here are some different outdoor gyms from around the world.

There is a famous outdoor gym called Muscle Beach in California, USA. Bodybuilders, weightlifters, athletes, and gymnasts train here. It's now a popular tourist attraction and you can buy a ticket to go see the place!

China has many outdoor gyms. This is the outdoor gym in the People's Park in Haikou. About 40% of China's 1.4 billion people use outdoor gyms regularly, according to Top.me. There are about 600,000 outdoor gyms in the country. They are all free!

A new outdoor gym in Sunnymead Park in Oxford, England, has some interesting technology. When people exercise on the machines, they create electricity. The electricity creates power for streetlights, smartphones, or tablets. Amazing!

Read more

1 Which gym can you pay money to visit?
2 How many outdoor gyms are there in China?
3 Where can you exercise to help the environment?

C IN PAIRS **Look at the pictures and answer the question.**

1 What parts of the body do you think the pieces of equipment are good for?

I think this equipment is good for the arms and the shoulders.

1
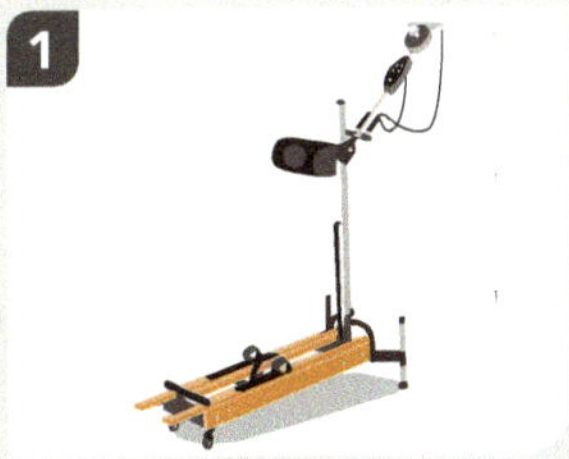
skier, $1,100

2

walker, $1,500

3

arm and leg bike, $900

4

waist twist, $1,080

5

two-person leg push, $1,110

6

two-person pull-down, $2,300

7
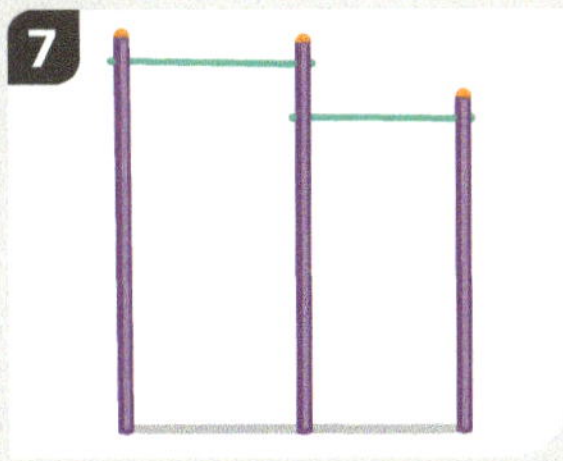
two-person pull-up, $2,300

D Read the email and answer the question.

1 What does the Director of Public Health want help with?

New Message

From: publichealth@gov.gov

To: citycouncil@gov.gov Cc Bcc

Subject: I need your ideas

Dear City Council Members,

We are looking at ways to help people be healthy in our city. We can have outdoor gyms in parks around the city. There is a budget of $8,000 for new gym equipment for one local park. People want equipment that is:

- for people of all ages
- easy to use
- good for different parts of the body

I look forward to hearing your ideas. Let me know what equipment is good for our park. Let's work together to create a great outdoor gym.

Regards,
The Director of Public Health

Send

E IN GROUPS **Imagine your group works for the city council. Look at the equipment in C. Work together to decide what to buy.**

A: I think we can get the … It's good for the …

B: I don't think we can get the … because it's expensive.
How about we get the … instead?

F Share your choices with the Director of Public Health. Explain why you like this equipment.

MAKE IT DIGITAL

Go online and find your nearest outdoor gym. What equipment does it have?

VOCABULARY review

SCORE: / 10

A **Choose the correct option.**

Almost New

Almost new fitness **1 pass / tracker**. Wear it on one **2 back / arm** while you **3 do / go** gymnastics, play **4 tennis / biking**, or any other sport. $55.

Used

Used exercise DVD. Do your daily **5 workout / kick** with trainer Danny Lee. Do **6 push-ups / baseball**, sit-ups, and other exercises to **7 get / cut** in shape fast. $10.

Almost New

Sports **8 fitness / camera**. Takes great pictures. I use it for water sports like **9 running / surfing** and swimming. Hold it in your **10 hand / shoulder** or wear it on your head. $150.

GRAMMAR review

SCORE: / 10

A **Match the sentence beginning (1–5) to the sentence end (a–e). Write the letter.**

1 She can't ____
2 Can you explain ____
3 Where can I ____
4 I can play ____
5 He can play soccer, ____

a volleyball and tennis.
b sing or dance.
c but he can't play rugby.
d the rules of cricket?
e buy tickets to the game?

B **Complete the sentences with the adverb form of the adjectives in parentheses.**

1 Baseball players need to run ____________ (fast) to first base after they hit the ball.
2 Good basketball players can score 20 to 30 points in a game ____________ (easy).
3 It's important for a rugby player to pass the ball ____________ (careful) to another player.
4 Volleyball players near the net often hit the ball ____________ (hard).
5 Soccer teams need to play ____________ (good) together to win.

16–20 correct: You can talk about parts of the body and exercise words. You can use *can/can't* and adverbs of manner.
0–15 correct: Look again at the Vocabulary and Grammar sections in the unit.

TOTAL SCORE: / 20

WHAT DO YOU KNOW NOW? Look back at page 67 and add the words you know now to the boxes.

STUDY SKILLS EFFECTIVE GROUP WORK

Take the quiz on effective group work. Go to **Study Skills** on page 133 to find the answers. Then learn more about effective group work.

1 **What kind of team performs best?**
a a mixed-age team **b** a young-people-only team **c** a men-only team

2 **You're in a meeting. Someone makes a suggestion you don't agree with. What do you say?**
a "Really? Ha, ha!" **b** "That's interesting. Why do you think that?" **c** "You're wrong."

3 **You're working in a group when you make a mistake. What do you say?**
a "I'm sorry, my mistake." **b** "Excuse me?" **c** nothing

4 **People who work alone get better results than small teams.**
a true **b** false

UNIT
8 Foodie?

WHAT DO YOU ALREADY KNOW?

1 Think of words for foods that are healthy and unhealthy. Write the words.

2 **IN PAIRS** Share and compare your information. Add more words to your lists.

Healthy

Unhealthy

DISCUSS & SHARE

VIDEO

3 **IN GROUPS** Watch the video and answer the question.

SYM Do you "eat to live" or "live to eat"?

In this unit, you will ...

- talk about food, tastes, ingredients, and recipes.
- use thinking skills: apply, analyze, and evaluate.
- read about international foods.
- use strategies to repair talking by checking for understanding.
- use communication skills to design a restaurant guide.
- follow a baker to learn about this job and the skills needed for this industry.

Are You a "Gastronaut"?

READING

A IN GROUPS **Look at the pictures. Do you know these foods? Do you want to try them? Discuss.**

hagelslag
(the Netherlands)

bunny chow
(South Africa)

empanadas
(Venezuela)

cendol
(Malaysia)

tom yum soup
(Thailand)

B 8.01 READING SKILL—Read for the main idea **Read the posts from a world food forum and answer the questions.**

Wendy, Canada, 5:34 says ...
Hi, food fans! Do you know the word *gastronaut*? It's a person who travels and tries different foods. That's me! I love something **delicious** called *hagelslag*. It's from the Netherlands. It has small, sweet pieces of chocolate you put on bread for breakfast. My boyfriend thinks it's **disgusting**! Do you like foods from different countries? What kind? How many new dishes do you try each week?

Soraya, Bali, 9:45 says ...
I'm a gastronaut, too! I love to try different foods from all over the world. My favorite food is *tom yum soup*, from Thailand. It's a spicy soup with shrimp and vegetables. I often have it for lunch. It's a very **healthy** meal! I add chilies to mine to make it extra spicy.

Peter, South Africa, 9:54 says ...
Hi, Wendy! Do you know about *bunny chow*? It comes from South Africa. It's a loaf of bread, but you take the middle of the bread out and put **spicy** beef or chicken inside. How much meat do you need? It depends on how big the loaf is! We usually eat it for lunch or dinner.

Marlena, Venezuela, 11:32 says ...
My favorite food is *empanadas*. They are delicious. You can make them with corn flour, water, and salt. You can put cheese, meat, chicken—anything you like—inside. Then, you fry them. Some people eat them as a **snack**. My mom thinks they are **unhealthy** because you fry them.

Ben, Scotland, 12:54 says ...
I think I'm a gastronaut, too. Do you know a dessert called *cendol* from Malaysia? It's really unusual. It's green rice noodles, coconut milk, and sugar. You can also add fruit. It's very **sweet**. It looks like green spaghetti!

1 What kind of flour do you use for empanadas? ______
2 What food is from Thailand? ______
3 Is bunny chow a snack? ______
4 What is cendol? ______
5 Are you a gastronaut? Why or why not? ______

C IN PAIRS THINKING SKILL—Apply **Think about a popular food in your country. What is it? When do you eat it? What is in it? Do you like it? Tell your partner.**

VOCABULARY

A **Find and circle all the food items in READING B.**

B **Match the underlined words in READING B to the definitions (1–7).**

1 has the hot taste of chilies (adjective) ____________
2 tastes very, very bad (adjective) ____________
3 good for your body (adjective) ____________
4 has the taste of sugar (adjective) ____________
5 a small amount of food you eat between meals (noun) ____________
6 not good for your body (adjective) ____________
7 has a very good taste (adjective) ____________

MAKE IT YOURS

Think about a food and a drink that you like. Use a dictionary to add the words to the vocabulary list for this lesson.

GRAMMAR countable and uncountable nouns

A **Complete the examples with the foods from READING B. Then complete the rules.**

Countable nouns

Singular: a vegetable, ____________, ____________, ____________

Plural: vegetables, ____________, ____________

Uncountable nouns

chocolate, *bread*, ____________, ____________, ____________, ____________

Questions

How many ____________? *How much* ____________?

1 Countable nouns are people or things you **can** / **can't** count. Use numbers and the article *a*/*an* with countable nouns.
2 Countable nouns can be **singular** / **plural** / **both singular and plural**.
3 Uncountable nouns are not **singular** / **plural**.
4 We use *How many ...?* with **countable** / **uncountable** nouns.
5 We use *How much ...?* with **countable** / **uncountable** nouns.

For more practice, go to page 152.

B **Complete with the singular or plural form of the noun.**

1 How much ____________ (milk) do you want in your coffee?
2 I like ____________ (banana) and ____________ (grape), but I don't like ____________ (orange).
3 Can I have ____________ (cheese) on my pizza, please?
4 How many ____________ (egg) do you want for breakfast?
5 I don't eat ____________ (fish) or meat. I'm a vegetarian.

SPEAKING

A **Make a list of foods you know from different countries in your notebook.**

B IN PAIRS **Ask and answer questions about the foods you like. Use the Confident Communicator box to help you.**

C **Take a class survey to see how many gastronauts are in your class. Discuss.**

CONFIDENT COMMUNICATOR
START TALKING

There are different ways to ask about preferences.
Do you like Thai food? Yes, I do. / No, I don't.
Which do you prefer, chicken or fish?
I prefer chicken (to fish).
Do you prefer pasta or rice? I prefer pasta.

A Balanced Diet

VOCABULARY food groups

A Look at the food group diagram. Complete the diagram with words from the box.

apples	bananas	beans	bread	butter	cereal	cheese	chocolate	corn	eggs
fish	ice cream	milk	oil	pasta	potatoes	rice	soda	chicken	yogurt

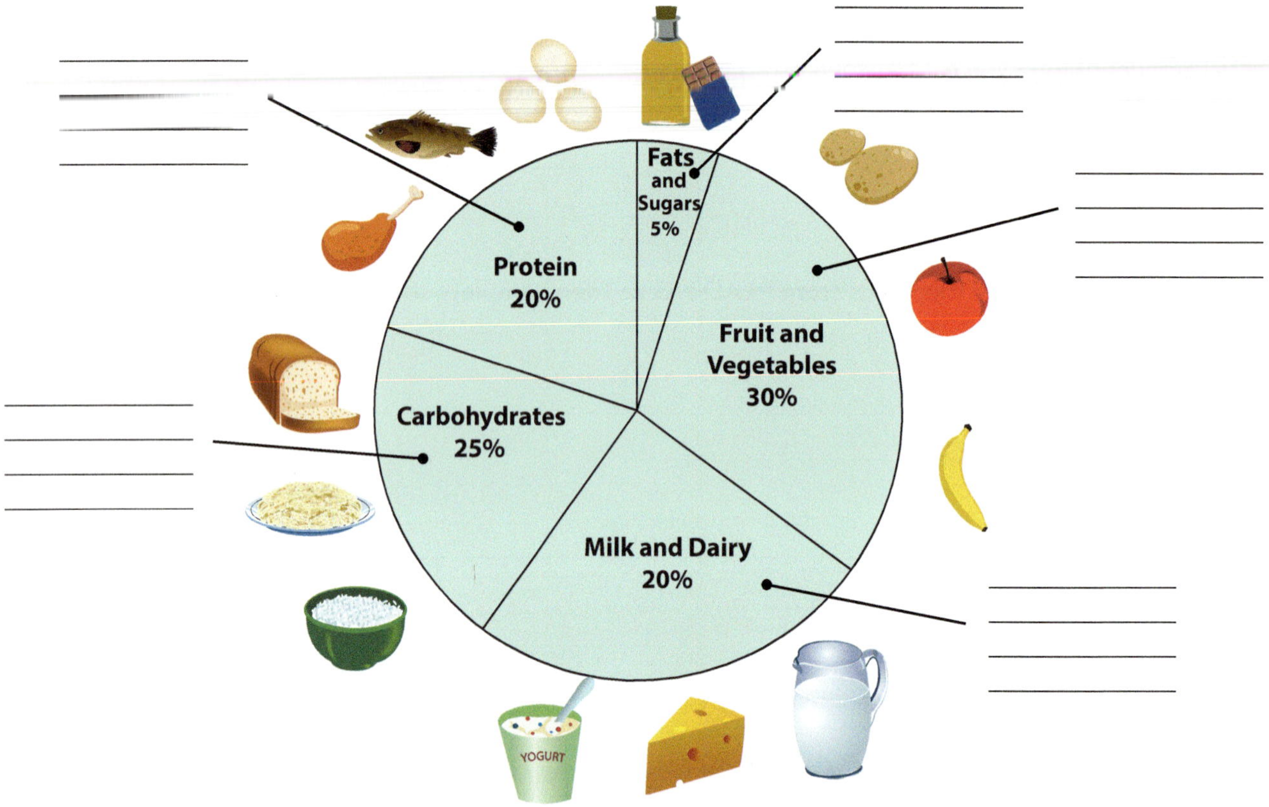

B IN PAIRS Discuss how much of each food group you eat.

I usually eat two kinds of protein a day, but I don't eat a lot of fruit and vegetables.

LISTENING

A Discuss the questions.

1 Do you like going to food markets?
2 What foods do you eat there?

B 8.02 Listen to Conversations 1 and 2 and choose *True* or *False*.

1 The interviewer thinks falafel is spicy. True / False
2 The woman says that her falafel is unhealthy. True / False
3 The bibimbap has carbohydrates, vegetables, and protein. True / False
4 The man's bibimbap is vegan. True / False

C 8.02 LISTENING SKILL—Listen for specific information Listen again and write the words you hear.

1 Food markets like this sell cheap food, but is it ______________?
2 This falafel is healthy because we grill it. Fried falafel has more ______________ and calories.
3 It looks like a/an ______________ meal!
4 So, the food at this market is ______________, and some of it is healthy, too.

D THINKING SKILL—Analyze Look up the words *vegan* and *vegetarian*. Do you think you can be vegan or vegetarian? Why or why not?

GRAMMAR *this/that/these/those*

A Read the conversation. Then complete the rules with *this/that* or *these/those*.

Shelly: Hi. Can I get a pound of apples, please?
Jon: Sure. Do you want those green ones?
Shelly: No, these apples, please. The red ones.
Jon: OK. Anything else?
Shelly: How big is that watermelon?
Jon: That one is small. It's 10 pounds.
Shelly: And this watermelon here?
Jon: This one is 15 pounds.
Shelly: OK, this one, please. Thanks.

1 Use ________ and ________ with singular nouns.
2 Use ________ and ________ with plural nouns.
3 Use ________ and ________ to talk about things near us.
4 Use ________ and ________ to talk about things not near us.

For more practice, go to page 153.

B Look at the pictures. Complete with *this*, *that*, *these*, or *those*.

1 
2 
3 
4 

1 Can we sit at ________ table, please?
2 Can I have ________ apples, please?
3 How much is ________?
4 I like ________. They're delicious.

PRONUNCIATION emphasis with *this/that/these/those*

A 8.03 Listen to the conversations. Underline the words the speakers stress.

Conversation 1
A: Is this my salad?
B: No, that's your salad.

Conversation 2
A: Are these your apples?
B: No, those are my apples.

Conversation 3
A: Do you want that snack?
B: No, I want this one.

B 8.03 Listen again and practice stressing the correct words.

SPEAKING

A IN PAIRS **Discuss the difference between healthy and unhealthy foods. Make a note of the healthy and unhealthy foods you eat every day.**

B IN GROUPS **Make a meal plan. Discuss and recommend healthy foods that your group can eat for every meal of the day. Use the Confident Communicator box to help you.**

A: Hmm. How about donuts for breakfast?
B: Well, they're very sweet.
A: How about cereal with fruit instead?
B: Yes, that's healthy.

CONFIDENT COMMUNICATOR
KEEP TALKING

It's a good idea to recommend an alternative when you give advice. Use *instead* (in place of).
How about + noun + *instead*?
e.g., *How about a sandwich instead?*

VOCABULARY cooking

A Match the words from the box to the pictures (1–10).

baking dish bowl measuring cup fork knife spoon add bake mix slice

1 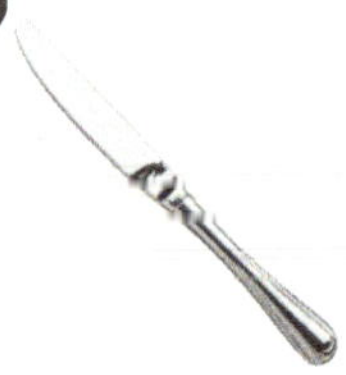 ______

2  ______

3  ______

4  ______

5  ______

6  ______

7  ______

8  ______

9  ______

10  ______

B Read the recipe for ice cream banana bread. Match the instructions (1–7) to the pictures (a–g). Write the letter.

Ice Cream Banana Bread

EASY, DELICIOUS, AND ONLY FIVE INGREDIENTS!

a 

b 

c 

d 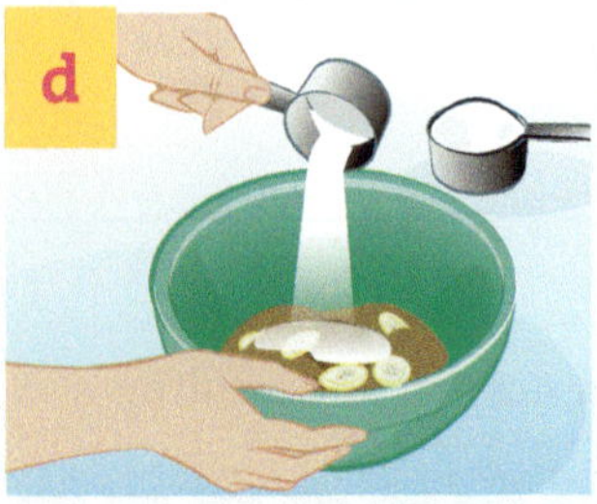

e 

f 

g 

Oil
3 bananas
1 cup of flour
¼ cup of sugar
2 cups of chocolate ice cream

Oven: 175 degrees Celsius
Cooking time: 1 hour

1 Pour the mixture into the baking dish. ______
2 Put oil on the baking dish. ______
3 Bake for one hour. ______
4 Slice the bananas. ______
5 Add the flour and sugar. ______
6 Mix again with a spoon. ______
7 Put the bananas and ice cream together in a bowl and mix with a fork. ______

C IN PAIRS Give instructions on making ice cream banana bread.

LISTENING

A **Do you cook? What do you make? Discuss as a class.**

B 8.04 LISTENING SKILL—Listen for specific information **Listen and complete the ingredient list.**

Rainbow Pizza (a snack for 4–6 people)

Ingredients

- 2 ____________ of flour
- oil
- 1 cup of water
- 1 orange ____________
- 1 cup of ____________
- 2 cups of ____________ cheese
- 1 cup of red tomatoes
- 1 green pepper
- _____ purple onion
- salt and pepper

C 8.05 **Listen and complete the instructions.**

1 Put the flour in a/an ____________. Add salt and pepper. Then add the water and oil.
2 ____________ with a spoon or fork. Then use your hands to make a ball. Roll the ball into a circle.
3 Put the pizza dough on a ____________.
4 ____________ all the vegetables into small pieces. Don't mix them together.
5 Put the ____________ on the pizza dough first.
6 Make a row of ____________, then orange peppers, then corn.
7 ____________, add green peppers. Then add purple onions.
8 ____________ at 200°C for 20 minutes. Then slice.

MAKE IT REAL

I'm starving! = *I am very hungry.*
I'm stuffed! = *I can't eat more food.*

D THINKING SKILL—Evaluate **Think about the questions.**

1 Do you think it's important how food looks?
2 Does food that looks good usually taste good?

WRITING

A **Think about food you like from your country. Choose one dish that you know how to make.**

B **List the ingredients in your notebook.**

C **Read the recipe from LISTENING C and underline the imperatives.**

D **Write your recipe in your notebook using imperatives.**

SPEAKING

A IN PAIRS **Play a game. Student A: Read the recipe slowly. Don't say the name of the dish. Student B: Guess the dish. Then change roles. Use the Confident Communicator box to help you.**

CONFIDENT COMMUNICATOR
REPAIR IT

Sometimes you need to ask someone to say something again to check your understanding. There are polite ways to say this:
Can you say that again, please?
Can you repeat that?
Can you say that more slowly, please?

Language and Life

Communication – A Restaurant Guide

A 8.06 **Read the reviews from a local restaurant guide. Do you want to try the restaurants? Why?**

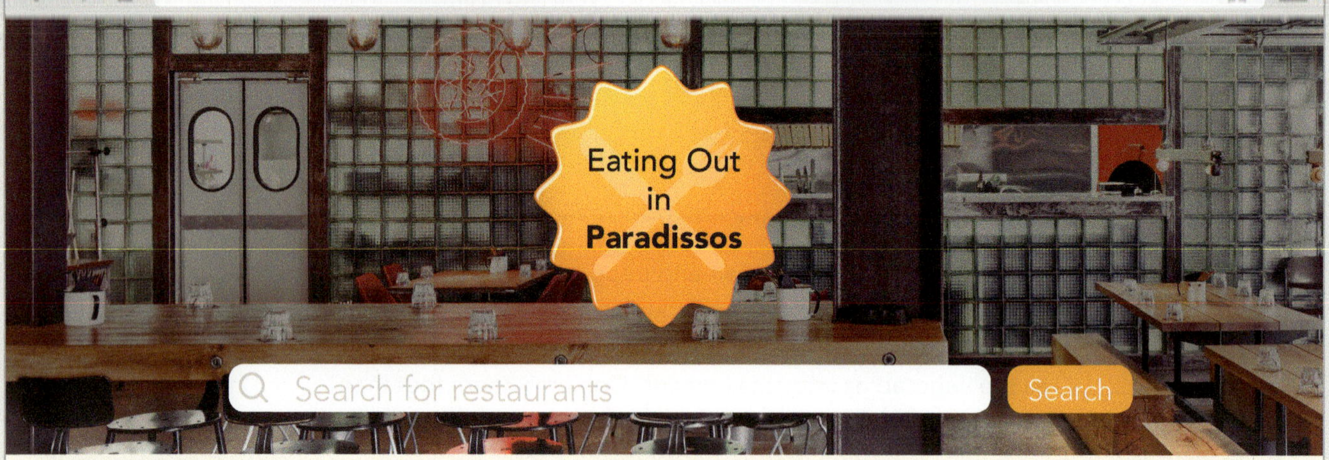

Many people like to eat out in a neighborhood called Paradissos. There are a lot of bars and restaurants, and food from around the world, like Thai, Japanese, Greek, French—you name it! Some of the restaurants are great for snacks, but there are some expensive restaurants, too. It's hard to know what's good and what's not, so here is our guide to the places we like in Paradissos …

Matilda's: vegetarian restaurant. Great for lunch. Healthy food.
We like: the mushroom burger and the delicious avocado salad
We don't like: the carrot cake, there are only five tables
$20 for lunch
★ ★ ★

Yu Garden: Chinese restaurant. Open evenings only.
We like: the chicken noodles and egg fried rice
We don't like: the noise, the open kitchen
$30 for 3 dishes
★ ★ ★ ★

Fred's Fish: fish and seafood restaurant. Lunch and dinner. Outdoor tables in the summer.
We like: spicy shrimp spaghetti with tomatoes
We don't like: the vegetable dishes, small portions
$40–$60
★ ★ ★ ½

Encore: French café and restaurant. Breakfast, lunch, and dinner.
We like: the steak and fries—so tasty!
We don't like: nothing—we love everything here!
$25 in the café, $70 in the restaurant
★ ★ ★ ★ ★

B **Read the reviews again and complete.**

Which restaurant …

1 is expensive? ______________

2 is not open in the daytime? ______________

3 is a good place for people who don't eat meat or fish? ______________

4 is a good place to eat outside? ______________

C Read the article and make notes about a restaurant you know.

Eating Out in **Paradissos**

Write Restaurant Reviews

Do you like eating out? Do you have a favorite restaurant? We are making an exciting new food guide for the restaurants in your area. We are looking for people like you to write the restaurant reviews. We pay $100 for every review we use.

- What's the name of the restaurant?
- What type of food does it have? (for example, French / Spanish / Chinese / breakfast / snacks / etc.)
- What do you like / not like about the restaurant?
- How much is a meal for two people?
- How many stars (out of 5) do you give it?

1 Restaurant name: ______
2 Type of food: ______
3 What you like: ______
4 What you don't like: ______
5 How much is a meal for two people?: ______
6 How many stars (out of 5)?: ______

D IN PAIRS Discuss your ideas.

E IN GROUPS Choose one restaurant using the group's notes. Write a review.

F Take a class survey. Choose a restaurant to recommend to a visitor to your area.

MAKE IT DIGITAL

Go online to look for a new dish for the restaurant to serve. Include pictures, prices, and some information about the dish to make people want to try it!

VOCABULARY review

SCORE: / 10

A Choose the word that does NOT belong.

1 Proteins: **steak** / **corn** / **beans**
2 Fats/Sugars: **oil** / **butter** / **eggs**
3 Fruits/Vegetables: **grapes** / **rice** / **carrots**
4 Carbohydrates: **beef** / **bread** / **cereal**
5 Milk/Dairy: **yogurt** / **raisins** / **cheese**
6 Meals: **dinner** / **snack** / **breakfast**
7 Cooking utensils: **spoon** / **knife** / **add**
8 Cooking verbs: **delicious** / **bake** / **mix**
9 Words to describe food: **sweet** / **tall** / **disgusting**
10 Healthy foods: **salad** / **apples** / **donut**

GRAMMAR review

SCORE: / 10

A Find and correct one error in each sentence.

1 For this recipe, you need two banana and four eggs. ____________
2 Use a fork to mash the bananas in bowl with the eggs. ____________
3 Pour into a pan with oils and cook on both sides. ____________
4 Cook on both sides and top with fruit or a chocolate. ____________
5 How much servings it makes is up to you! ____________

B Choose the correct option.

1 Excuse me, but is **that** / **these** / **those** a vegetarian dish?
2 **These** / **This** / **Those** soup tastes delicious. Try it!
3 Waiter! **These** / **Those** / **This** vegetables don't taste good.
4 How much are **these** / **those** / **that** carrots over there?
5 Can you help me put **this** / **that** / **these** watermelon in my bag?

16–20 correct: You can talk about food and food groups. You can use countable/uncountable nouns and *this/that/these/those*.
0–15 correct: Look again at the Vocabulary and Grammar sections in the unit.

TOTAL SCORE: / 20

WHAT DO YOU KNOW NOW? Look back at page 77 and add the words you know now to the boxes.

FOLLOW A PRO FOOD INDUSTRY

Take the quiz about food stylists. Go to **Follow A Pro** on page 134 to find the answers. Then learn more about the food industry.

1 When food stylists take pictures of breakfast cereal, what do they use instead of milk?
a white glue **b** white toothpaste **c** cream

2 Food stylists use hand soap for the top of a cappuccino.
a true **b** false

3 What do food stylists do before they photograph a roast chicken?
a put newspaper inside it **b** paint it yellow **c** cover it with nail polish

4 Food stylists use a special machine to add sesame seeds to hamburger buns.
a true **b** false

UNIT
9 Seeing the World

WHAT DO YOU ALREADY KNOW?

1 **Think about words you know about tourism and travel. Write the words.**

2 **IN PAIRS** **Share and compare your information. Add more words to your list.**

Travel and Tourism

VIDEO

DISCUSS & SHARE

3 **IN GROUPS** **Watch the video and answer the question.**

SYM Is tourism good or bad?

In this unit, you will ...

- talk about travel, make travel recommendations, and give advice on packing.
- use thinking skills: analyze, recall, and infer.
- read about virtual travel.
- use strategies to start and keep talking by taking time to think and asking follow-up questions.
- use collaboration skills to work as a team and create an advertisement to attract tourists.
- learn tips for formal and informal writing.

Virtual Tours

READING

A **You can go anywhere in the world. Where do you want to go? Discuss as a class.**

B 9.01 **Read the article and choose *True* or *False*.**

There but Not There: Virtual Travel

Would you like to visit another **continent**—Europe, maybe? See Italy or Greece? Or how about a country in Africa, like Kenya? If you want to save time and money when you travel, here's a tip. You need to try virtual tourism! But what is virtual tourism? And how does it work?

When you plan to visit a new place, go online and take a virtual tour first. You can use a virtual reality headset and a computer to take a **tour**. You don't have to use a computer if you have an app on your smartphone.

A virtual tour gives you all the **sights** and **sounds** of a place. Take a tour of a street market in a city like Delhi or enjoy **tourist attractions** in Rio de Janeiro. You can decide what you like to do before you go.

Many people enjoy traveling more when they plan with virtual tours. They like spending time on things that interest them. With virtual tours, they can spend more time on the things they love when they finally get to their dream **vacation** destination!

1 Virtual tourism is only for people with a lot of money. True / False
2 On a virtual tour, you can see and hear a place. True / False
3 You need a computer to take a virtual tour. True / False
4 A virtual tour can help you decide where to go. True / False

C READING SKILL—Scan **Scan the text and complete.**

1 Continents: ____________, ____________
2 Countries: ____________, ____________, ____________
3 Cities: ____________, ____________

D THINKING SKILL—Analyze **Answer the questions.**

1 How does a virtual tour save you time and money?
2 Is taking a virtual tour a good idea? Why or why not?

VOCABULARY

A **Match the words and phrases (1–6) to the definitions (a–f). Write the letter.**

1 continent ____
2 sights ____
3 sounds ____
4 tour ____
5 tourist attractions ____
6 vacation ____

a places tourists visit
b a trip around a place to see interesting things
c things you see
d a trip to another place, usually to relax
e large area of land, e.g., North America
f things you hear

GRAMMAR verb + infinitive or gerund

A **Complete with phrases from READING B.**

1 ____________ you ____________ another continent—Europe, maybe?
2 If you ____________ time and money, here's a tip.
3 You ____________ virtual tourism!
4 You can decide what you ____________ before you go.
5 Many people ____________ more when they plan with virtual tours.
6 They ____________ time on things that interest them.

B **Choose the correct option to complete the grammar rules.**

to go = infinitive	*go* = base form	*going* = *–ing* form

1 After *want*, *would like*, *need*, *have*, and *plan*, use the infinitive / base form.
2 After *enjoy*, use the infinitive / *–ing* form of verb.
3 After *like*, we can use the infinitive / *–ing* form of the verb / both.

For more practice, go to page 154.

C **Write sentences that are true for you.**

1 want / don't want … visit Europe / visit Africa
I want to visit Europe. I don't want to visit Africa.

2 would like / wouldn't like … visit a big city / visit a small village

3 like / don't like … travel by boat / travel by bus

4 enjoy / don't enjoy … visit new places / go to places I know

D **IN PAIRS Ask and answer questions about your sentences.**

A: Do you want to visit Europe?
B: Yes, I do. But I don't want to visit Africa.
A: I want to visit Europe and I want to visit Africa!

PRONUNCIATION *to*

A **9.02 Listen and notice how *to* sounds like /tə/.**

I want to visit Europe.
Do you like to travel?
I don't have to work on Monday.

B **9.02 Listen again and practice saying the sentences.**

SPEAKING

A **Plan a virtual tour.**

Where do you want to go? What do you want to see? Choose a place from the unit or use your own ideas.

B **Write why you want to visit that place and see that sight in your notebook.**

I want to go to Sydney, Australia, and see Bondi Beach because I like to swim.

C **IN PAIRS Student A, ask Student B about his or her virtual tour choices. Use phrases and short questions to show you are interested. Then change roles. Use the Confident Communicator box to help you.**

Where do you want to go on a virtual tour?
What do you want to do there?

CONFIDENT COMMUNICATOR
KEEP TALKING

Take time to think about what you want to say and how you want to say it. Use words and sounds like:
Um …
Uh …
Let me think …

LESSON 2 Travel Advice

LISTENING

A IN PAIRS **Discuss if you like to visit a place during high tourist season or low tourist season. Write advantages and disadvantages for each.**

high season

1 Advantages: good weather, ______
2 Disadvantages: lots of people, ______

low season

3 Advantages: quiet, ______
4 Disadvantages: bad weather, ______

B 9.03 **Listen to part of a radio show. Decide whether each speaker prefers high season or low season.**

	high season	low season
1 Manuel	☐	☐
2 Andra	☐	☐
3 Viktor	☐	☐

C 9.03 LISTENING SKILL—Listen for detail **Listen again and write the words you hear.**

1 Manuel: I like the winter, ______.
2 Andra: My favorite time of year is the ______.
3 Viktor: We get tourists all year, but the high season is ______.

D IN PAIRS THINKING SKILL—Recall **Two of the speakers prefer the high season. Can you remember the two reasons?**

VOCABULARY tourism collocations

A **Check (✓) the things you like to do when you visit a place.**

1 buy a souvenir

2 stay at a hotel

3 see the sights

4 take a taxi/bus

5 take a trip

6 take a guided tour

B **Complete the email with phrases from A.**

New Message

From: David Alegre, tour operator — Cc Bcc

To: Erin Rogers — Cc Bcc

Subject: Your trip to our city

Dear Erin,

Thanks for your email and the questions about our city. The high season is December to March. It's a good time to **1** ______________ to the area if you like lots of people. When you come, you can **2** ______________ on Copacabana Beach. There are lots of hotels on the beach. It's a good idea to **3** ______________ around the city with one of our tour guides. That way, you can **4** ______________, such as Sugar Loaf Mountain. If you prefer to explore on your own, **5** ______________ to Corcovado. From there, you can see the city, and of course you can **6** ______________ of your visit there. We look forward to seeing you in our city!

Best wishes,
David Alegre

Send

C **Discuss what tourists do when they visit your town or city. Use phrases from A.**

GRAMMAR *should/could* for advice and possibility

A **Read the sentences from the radio show. Then choose the correct option to complete the grammar rules.**

Manuel: Tourists are good for the economy. We should welcome them.
Lucia: We could get more tourists by opening more hotels.

1 Use *should* + **base form of the verb** / **infinitive** to talk about things that are *important* for people to do (advice).
2 Use *could* + **base form of the verb** / **infinitive** to talk about things that are *possible* for people to do (possibility).

For more practice, go to page 154.

B **Complete with *could* or *should* and the verb given.**

1 You ______________ to China! Or maybe India! They're both interesting. (go / possibility)
2 You ______________ some warm clothes. It can be cold in Sweden! (pack / advice)
3 You need to rest. You ______________ on vacation. (go / advice)
4 Alex ______________ a taxi, or maybe a bus to get downtown. (take / possibility)

C IN PAIRS **Make a list of what a good tourist *should* or *could* do in your notebook.**

SPEAKING

A IN PAIRS **Role-play a conversation. Use the Confident Communicator box to help you.**

Student A: You want to take a vacation. Ask questions about your partner's country or city.
Student B: You are a tour operator. Sell a tour to your partner.

A: Hello. I'm going on vacation next summer and I want to visit your country. I want to take a trip, but I don't know where.
B: You could go to … because …

CONFIDENT COMMUNICATOR
KEEP TALKING

There are two ways to make suggestions:
*You **could** take a virtual tour.*
***Why don't you** take a virtual tour?*

What to Pack

VOCABULARY clothes

A Look at the pictures. Write the names of the clothing items using a dictionary.

1	________	6	________	11	________	16	________
2	________	7	________	12	________	17	________
3	________	8	________	13	________	18	________
4	________	9	________	14	________	19	________
5	________	10	________	15	________	20	________

LISTENING

A IN PAIRS Ask and answer questions about what you should pack for a short trip to a warm country and a short trip to a cold country.

B 9.04 LISTENING SKILL—Listen for gist Listen and choose the correct option.

1 José travels on vacation / for work.
2 Isabela enjoys swimming / hiking on vacation.
3 Mike likes swimming / hiking on vacation.
4 Amal likes to visit beaches / cities.

C 9.04 Listen again and complete. What do the speakers pack?

1 José: ________, ________
2 Isabela: ________, ________
3 Mike: ________, ________
4 Amal: ________, ________

D THINKING SKILL—Deduce Match the speakers (1–4) to another destination (a–d). Write the letter. Discuss why it's a good place for him/her.

1 José ____
2 Isabela ____
3 Mike ____
4 Amal ____

a Greenland
b New York
c Chile
d Spain

MAKE IT YOURS

Use a dictionary to find words for clothes that you are wearing now or that you usually wear.

WRITING

A **Read the tourism pamphlet. Then think about the climate in your area.**

Before you book your trip to Thailand with Thai Tours, we'd like to share some information.

During the cool season (November to February), temperatures in the central region are about 21°C and 14°C in the north. You should pack some warm clothes, such as a sweater or a sweatshirt. During the hot season (March to June), temperatures are between 34°C and 40°C. You need summer clothes, such as shorts, T-shirts, and your swimsuit! The rainy season is from July to October. It's very wet! You should pack a hat and a raincoat.

We look forward to welcoming you to Thailand!

B **Plan your writing. Complete the notes for your area.**

My area: __________

High-season climate: __________

What to pack: __________

Low-season climate: __________

What to pack: __________

C **Write information for tourists visiting your area. Give them advice on what to pack for different times of the year.**

SPEAKING

A **Look at the different vacations. Choose the one you like best.**

1 an adventure vacation

2 a beach vacation

3 a hiking vacation

4 a sightseeing vacation

B **You are going on that vacation! Where are you going? What is the climate like there? Write four things you need to pack for your trip in your notebook.**

C **IN PAIRS Discuss the trip you are planning. Say what you are taking with you and why. Use the Confident Communicator box to help you.**

CONFIDENT COMMUNICATOR
START TALKING

Ask your partner these questions:
What kind of trip are you going on?
Why do you like that kind of trip?
What are you taking with you? Why are you taking that?

Language and Life

Collaboration – Detourism

A 9.05 IN PAIRS **Read the text and discuss the questions.**

DETOURISM

Love or hate it, Venice is a very popular tourist destination. Some people say it's too popular! Around 30 million people visit Venice, Italy, every year. The problem is, they all want to see the same things: the canals, St. Mark's Square, the Doge's Palace. The small city of Venice (population 50,000) attracts large crowds of visitors every year. Tourism is important for the economy of the city, but it's very expensive to keep Venice in good condition.

To deal with this problem, some people suggest detourism. A detour is a short trip in a different direction. Detourism shows tourists attractions that most people don't visit. That way, tourists aren't always in the same place at the same time. For example, when you move away from the canals, Venice also has interesting markets, restaurants, and shops. And there are unusual attractions, such as the multicolored houses on the island of Burano and the Lazzaretto Nuovo, home to the Vampire of Venice! It's a very different side of Venice.

Detourism can lead to many different kinds of vacations and new experiences. Have fun!

Read more

1 What problems does Venice have?

2 What do some people recommend?

B **Read the announcement and answer the questions.**

TOURISM COMPETITION

Win a weekend vacation for two!

Our area attracts many tourists every year. Most of the tourists are families, but we want to attract more English-speaking young adults to the area, too. We want them to visit our main attractions, but we need to tell them about the many interesting things in our area. Do you have any ideas how to do that? If so, enter the Tourism Competition. You could design a poster, or perhaps you could make a short video. You could also make a slideshow or design a special tour of our area. Choose anything that works for you!

Send your entry to the Local Tourist Office, 135 Main St.

1 What could you win in this competition? ______

2 Who does the Tourist Office want to attract? ______

3 What could you create? ______

C **IN GROUPS** **Decide what you want to create. Choose or add your own ideas.**

a poster
a video
a slideshow
a tour

D **Make a list of tourist attractions in your area. Then choose attractions for your competition entry.**

famous attractions

____
____
____

natural attractions

____
____
____

other attractions (detourism!)

____
____
____

E **Choose three attractions and make notes.**

	Attraction 1	Attraction 2	Attraction 3
What is the attraction?			
What can you do there?			
Why do young adults like it?			

F **Read the advice and create your competition entry.**

TOURISM COMPETITION

Competition entries

A poster
Find some nice pictures of your area. Think about where you want to put the information on your poster. Use topics to interest people.

A slideshow
Find some nice pictures of your area. Use a different slide for each attraction. Include key information. Perhaps include a link to an online video.

A video
Decide who is doing what (such as filming and presenting). Write a short script. Film the tourism video on your smartphone. You can film the attractions!

A tour
Think about some unusual tourist attractions in your area. Think about what young people like to do and see. Write a description of each place on your tour. Find some nice pictures of your area to add to the tour.

G **Share your competition entry with the class.**

MAKE IT DIGITAL

Search online for a detourism tour of a city you are interested in. Tell your class about the tour.

VOCABULARY review

SCORE: / 10

A Complete the definitions with the words in the box.

continent	guided	hotel	scarf	sights
gloves	hat	market	sneakers	souvenirs

1 ________ : you wear these on your hands
2 ________ : you wear this around your neck
3 ________ : you wear these on your feet
4 ________ : you wear this on your head
5 ________ : you buy these on a trip
6 ________ : you stay here on a trip
7 ________ : Africa is an example of this
8 ________ : you see these on a tour
9 ________ : a place to buy things
10 ________ : a type of tour

GRAMMAR review

SCORE: / 10

A Choose the correct option.

Tom: I **1** want / enjoy to visit Ecuador this summer. I **2** enjoy / would hiking and shopping. I **3** have / would like to stay in Quito and visit some small towns as day tours. Is this a good idea?

Ana: I live in Quito, and summer here is very nice. You **4** like / have to visit Otavalo! There's great shopping there. **5** Plan / Want to go on Saturday—the market is very busy then.

B Complete the sentences with *could* or *should* and a word from the box.

eat	go	remember	take	visit

1 I think you ________ Korea in the autumn. It's the best time to visit.
2 There are different ways to get around. You ________ trains, buses, or even planes.
3 You ________ in a big hotel, but think about a small family-run restaurant.
4 Do you like hiking? You ________ to Seoraksan, or maybe Jirisan.
5 Korea can be cold in October. You ________ to pack a jacket.

16–20 correct: You can talk about travel, tourism, and clothes. You can use verb + infinite or gerund and *should/could*.
0–15 correct: Look again at the Vocabulary and Grammar sections in the unit.

TOTAL SCORE: / 20

WHAT DO YOU KNOW NOW? Look back at page 87 and add the words you know now to the box.

STUDY SKILLS FORMAL AND INFORMAL WRITING

Take the quiz about writing skills. Go to **Study Skills** on page 135 to find the answers. Then learn more about formal and informal writing.

1 We often use slang expressions (e.g., *cool*, *kid*, *chill out*) in …
a formal writing. **b** informal writing.

2 Which of these sentences is from a formal piece of writing?
a Soccer is a popular sport in Brazil. **b** Soccer is awesome—I love it!

3 Contractions (*I'm*, *don't*, *who's*) are usually used in …
a formal writing. **b** informal writing.

4 How do you start a formal letter?
a Dear … **b** Hi …

UNIT 10 Life Stories

WHAT DO YOU ALREADY KNOW?

1 **Think about the last ten photos you took on your phone. Make a list of the photos.**
2 **IN PAIRS Share and compare your photos. Add more words to your list.**

Last 10 photos on my phone

DISCUSS & SHARE

VIDEO

3 **IN GROUPS Watch the video and answer the question.**
SYM How much of your life do you put online?

In this unit, you will ...

- talk about life events, social life, and personal experiences.
- use thinking skills: summarize, evaluate, and analyze.
- read about a famous person.
- use strategies to keep talking by showing interest.
- use empathy skills to give advice based on your own experience.
- read about an event organizer to learn about this job and the skills needed for the tourism industry.

LESSON 1 A Brave Life

READING

A **Look at the picture. Do you know anything about this person? Why do you think she is famous?**

B 10.01 **Read the biography. Then complete the sentences.**

An Inspiration For All

Malala Yousafzai was born in 1997 in the Swat Valley in Pakistan. Her father was an educator, and he wanted his daughter to get an education, but in 2007 and 2008, the schools for girls closed in her region of Pakistan, and Malala stopped going to school.

Malala wrote a **blog** for British TV about her life that year. She wanted all girls to have the opportunity to get an education. She became **well known** in Pakistan. Then in 2011, Malala's school finally opened again. Malala's blog made some powerful people angry. On October 9, 2012, Malala was shot on her way to school. She was only 14 years old.

Malala was lucky. She survived, and her family took her to England. When she was better, she started school there. She continued to talk about education for girls in Pakistan, and she went around the world to speak. In 2013, she started the Malala Fund. In 2014, she won the Nobel Peace Prize. The next year, a film of her life, called *He Named Me Malala*, told her story. In spring 2017, she went around the world on her Girl Power Trip and met world leaders. She asked them to support education for all girls. In autumn 2017, she started to study for a **degree** at Oxford University.

Malala continues to **inspire** young people around the world.

1 In 2008, Malala's ______________ closed.
2 She wrote ______________ about her life for British TV and became well known.
3 Malala was shot on her way to ______________.
4 She met ______________ when she traveled around the world in 2017.

MAKE IT YOURS

Find the life story of a person who inspires you. Use a dictionary to find the vocabulary you need to tell his or her life story to the class.

C **READING SKILL—Scan for information** **Put the milestones of Malala's life in the correct order. Write in your notebook.**

D **THINKING SKILL—Summarize** **Say what happened in Malala's life. Connect your ideas using *then*, *next*, and *after that*.**

VOCABULARY

A **Match the words and phrases (1–4) to the definitions (a–d). Write the letter.**

1 blog ____
2 well known ____
3 degree ____
4 inspire ____

a a website where people write their opinions
b what you get from a university, for example, Bachelor of Arts
c influence or motivate people
d famous or popular

GRAMMAR simple past (affirmative statements)

A **Read the text in READING B again. Complete with the simple past form of the verbs.**

Regular Verbs

1 start ______________ 2 continue ______________ 3 stop ______________ 4 open ______________

B Complete the table.

Spelling Changes for the Simple Past		
Regular verbs Example: *ask*	Add **1** ____________.	*asked*
Verbs ending in –*e* Example: *live*	Add **2** ____________.	*lived*
Verbs ending in vowel + consonant Example: *stop*	Double the last **3** ______ and add *–ed.*	*stopped*
Verbs ending in consonant + –*y* Example: *cry*	Change *y* to **4** ______ and add *–ed.*	*cried*

For more practice, go to page 155.

C Read the text in READING B again. Write the simple past form of the irregular verbs.

1 have ____________ **2** go ____________ **3** become ____________ **4** meet ____________

D Complete the conversation with the past tense of the verbs.

Logan: Who's that in the picture?

Chase: Oh, that's my grandfather. He **1** ____________ (be) born in 1940. He **2** ____________ (die) a few years ago. He **3** ____________ (have) an interesting life. He **4** ____________ (become) an engineer. He **5** ____________ (start) his own business and **6** ____________ (go) around the world. He **7** ____________ (meet) my grandmother in Spain and they **8** ____________ (marry) in 1970.

PRONUNCIATION the ending *–ed*

A Read the pronunciation rules. How do you think the words are pronounced?

voiced consonant + *–ed* = /d/	unvoiced consonant + *–ed* = /t/	verb ends in *t* or *d* + *–ed* = /ɪd/
learned	stopped	decided

B 10.02 Listen and check. Practice saying the verbs.

SPEAKING

A Write sentences about milestones in your life in your notebook.

B IN PAIRS Discuss. Use the Confident Communicator box to help you.

Choose three milestones and tell your partner about them. Then find another pair and tell them what you learned about each other.

CONFIDENT COMMUNICATOR
START TALKING

To talk about milestones, use *when I was* and your age at the time: *I learned to walk* ***when I was*** *10 months old.* You can also say the year and then your age: *I graduated from elementary school in 2013, when I was 12.*

LESSON 2 Social Life

VOCABULARY social life collocations

A Check (✓) things you did in the last month.

go out dancing ☐
have a party ☐
hang out with friends ☐
see a movie ☐
eat out at a restaurant ☐
go to a concert ☐
go on a date ☐
visit family ☐

B IN PAIRS Discuss your social life.

I ate out at a restaurant.
I saw a movie.
I met up with friends and I visited family. And you?

GRAMMAR simple past (negative statements and questions)

A Read the conversation. Underline a negative statement, a *yes/no* question, an information question, and a short answer. Then complete the rules.

Caleb: What did you do last night?
Ryan: I went out with friends. Did you go out?
Caleb: No, I didn't. I didn't want to go out. I stayed home and watched TV.

1 For negative statements, use ______ + the base form of the verb.
2 For *yes/no* questions, use ______ + subject + the base form of the verb.
3 For short answers, use *Yes* + subject + *did*, or *No* + subject + ______.
4 For *wh–* questions, use a question word + ______ + subject + the base form of the verb.

For more practice, go to page 156.

B Complete the conversation with an affirmative or negative form of the simple past.

Ryan: What **1** ______ you watch on TV?
Caleb: I watched a movie. **2** ______ you eat out at a restaurant?
Ryan: Yes, we **3** ______. We went to Luigi's.
Caleb: What **4** ______ you have?
Ryan: I **5** ______ hungry, so I **6** ______ order a lot. I just had a small pizza.

C IN PAIRS Ask your partner what he or she did last night.

A: What did you do last night? *B: I watched TV.*
A: What did you watch?

LISTENING

A **Look at the pictures. What do you think the LISTENING is about?**

B 10.03 LISTENING SKILL—Listen for main ideas **Listen to the conversation. Choose the things that the speakers talk about.**

order food	☐	have a party	☐
go on a date	☐	meet up with friends	☐
go out to eat	☐	see a movie	☐
go to a club	☐	visit family	☐

C 10.03 **Listen again, and write the reasons each person gives. Then check.**

1 Madison: I met up with friends because __________.
2 Madison: We went out to eat because __________.
3 Luciana: I didn't go out because __________.
4 Luciana: I ordered a pizza because __________.

D THINKING SKILL—Evaluate **Is it important to you to have a lot of friends, or do you prefer one or two close friends? Why?**

SPEAKING

A **Choose a topic to ask your partner about.**

what you did last weekend	☐	what you did last summer	☐
the last time you had fun	☐	the last time you found something	☐
the last time you ate out	☐	the last time you forgot something	☐

B IN PAIRS **Ask each other about your topics. Ask questions to learn more. Use the Confident Communicator box to help you.**

C **Tell the class what you learned about your partner.**

CONFIDENT COMMUNICATOR

KEEP TALKING

To encourage someone to say more:
Really?
Tell me about it. *So, what did you do?*
Tell me more. *Then what happened?*

In My Experience

VOCABULARY collocations with *get, have,* and *make*

A Look at the pictures. Write which situations are positive experiences, which are negative experiences, and which can be positive *and* negative.

1 
make a mistake

____

2 
get upset

____

3 
make a new friend

____

4 
have an argument

____

5 
make a decision

____

6 
have fun

____

7 
get lost

____

B Complete the conversation. Use phrases from A.

How was last night? Did you have **1** ______________ at the club?

Yes, we did. But at first Zac and I went to the wrong place! We got **2** ______________!

Oh, no! How did you make a **3** ______________ like that?

I don't know! I thought Zac knew the location. But we didn't get **4** ______________ or have an **5** ______________. We asked a woman and finally found the club. It's a great place!

LISTENING

A 10.04 LISTENING SKILL—Listen for gist Listen and choose the correct option.

1 Kristina is talking about a time when she …
a forgot something. **b** made a decision. **c** got upset.

2 Javier is talking about a time when he …
a had an argument. **b** got lost. **c** made a new friend.

3 Lauren is talking about a time when she …
a had an argument. **b** found something. **c** made a mistake.

B 10.04 Listen again and complete with the words you hear.

1 Kristina: I ______________ it was just a regular party, but it was her birthday, and I ______________!

2 Javier: When I ______________ him, I ______________ him where to go.

3 Lauren: When we ______________ there, they said they ______________ a table for us.

C THINKING SKILL—Analyze Compare the stories in the LISTENING to your life. Did anything like these experiences happen to you? Tell a partner.

WRITING

A Read the email. Choose *True* or *False*.

New Message

From: Juana@email.cc Cc Bcc

To: avery@email.cc Cc Bcc

Hi, Avery.

How are things?

The business trip to London was great, but I made a big mistake!

I went to a new restaurant with some friends. We had a good meal, but when we left, a car almost hit me outside the restaurant! I looked left, then right, before I crossed the street. But it's London! You have to look right, then left. Fortunately, the driver stopped in time, but we were both a little scared. He shouted at me to look both ways and drove away.

The next day, I went to the London office and guess what? I met the driver! He's one of my coworkers. In the end, we laughed about our "meeting" the day before. He's a really nice guy.

Write me soon with all your news!

Take care,

Juana

Send

1 Juana liked the restaurant. True / False
2 A car hit Juana. True / False
3 Juana had an argument with the driver. True / False
4 Juana met the driver again later. True / False
5 Juana and the driver are coworkers. True / False

MAKE IT YOURS

Business emails often include some personal experiences. When you describe some of your experiences, you connect with the people you work with.

B Write an email to a friend about a time you made a mistake, got lost, or had an argument. Use *first, next, later,* and *in the end.*

1 When did this happen? ______
2 What happened first? ______
3 What happened next / later / the next day? ______
4 What happened in the end? ______

SPEAKING

A Choose one of the experiences and think about a time when it happened to you. What happened? Make notes to help you.

- a time when I got upset
- a time when I had fun
- a time when I lost something important
- a time when I made a new friend

B IN PAIRS Role play. Student A, tell your partner about your experience. Student B, listen carefully to your partner, and ask any questions you have. Then change roles. Use the Confident Communicator box to help you.

CONFIDENT COMMUNICATOR
START TALKING

To say when something happened, use *yesterday, the day before yesterday,* or *last Monday / week / month / year,* etc.
You can also use a period of time + *ago:*
This happened two years ago.

Language and Life

Empathy – Take My Advice

A 10.05 **Read the web page. Then answer the questions.**

THE WORLD ADVICE CORNER

The world's problem-solving web page

Got a problem? Got a solution? Here at the World Advice Corner, we want you to use your experience to help each other. Post your problem and then read the advice from people around the world. Or find a problem and give your advice. Here's a selection of problems on the World Advice Corner.

My problem is that I'm lonely. It's hard to make new friends. I went to a party recently and spent most of the night in the kitchen! I get nervous around people I don't know. Does anyone have any advice? –Adrian

Submit Advice

My parents try to control my life! When I go out with friends, they always want to know exactly where I am and what I'm doing. I have to text them every half an hour or they worry. How can I find a solution? I don't want to argue with them. –Maria

Submit Advice

I have a work problem. Last week, I made a mistake and my boss yelled at me. I got upset and didn't know what to do. Did this ever happen to you? What did you do? All advice is welcome! –Olivia

Submit Advice

1 What happens on the advice website? ______
2 What problem does Adrian have? ______
3 What problem does Maria have? ______
4 What problem does Olivia have? ______

B IN GROUPS Discuss whether you have the same problem. Explain what happened.

I had the same problem as Olivia. I had an argument with my boss. She said …

C Read and choose the advice you think best fits each person.

1 What should Adrian do?
   a go to more parties **b** find a hobby **c** play a sport
2 What should Maria do?
   a explain how she feels **b** forget her parents and do what she wants **c** ask her parents to explain why they worry
3 What should Olivia do?
   a get another job **b** argue with her boss **c** explain to her boss how she feels

D **Make notes on advice for Adrian, Maria, and Olivia.**

I think Adrian should find a hobby because he can meet people with the same hobby.

Adrian: ____

____

Maria: ____

____

Olivia: ____

____

E **IN PAIRS Choose one person from D and write a complete post with your advice.**

Hi, Adrian. It's often hard to make friends, but here's our advice. First, find a hobby you like …

Submit Advice

____

____

____

____

____

F **Share your advice with the class. Take a class vote for the best advice.**

MAKE IT DIGITAL

Find an advice website like the one in the text. Submit a problem you have or one of the problems from **A**. See what advice you receive.

VOCABULARY review

SCORE: / 10

A Match the sentence beginning (1–10) to the sentence end (a–j). Write the letter.

1 Do you want to go on ____
2 Where do you usually meet up ____
3 How often do you go ____
4 At what age did you start ____
5 When did you last ____
6 How do your friends like to have ____
7 What makes you get ____
8 Would you like to watch ____
9 How often do you eat ____
10 In what year were you ____

a make a mistake?
b dancing?
c with friends?
d a date?
e school?
f out at a restaurant?
g a movie?
h fun?
i born?
j upset?

GRAMMAR review

SCORE: / 10

A Complete the paragraph with the simple past form of the verbs in parentheses.

In 2017, 16-year-old student Rayouf Alhumedhi **1** ________ (write) a text message to a friend. She **2** ________ (try) to add an emoji, but she **3** ________ (do not see) any on her phone that she **4** ________ (like). They **5** ________ (not look) like her. Alhumedhi, a Muslim from Saudi Arabia, **6** ________ (want) an emoji with a headscarf. So what **7** ________ she ________ (do)? She **8** ________ (ask) Apple and the Unicode emoji committee to make one. "It's something important to my identity," she **9** ________ (tell) *Time Magazine*. Apple soon **10** ________ (have) the new emoji on all its phones.

16–20 correct: You can talk about social life with *get, have,* and *make*. You can use the simple past in affirmative and negative statements.
0–15 correct: Look again at the Vocabulary and Grammar sections in the unit.

TOTAL SCORE: / 20

WHAT DO YOU KNOW NOW? Look back at page 97 and add the words you know now to the box.

FOLLOW A PRO EVENT PLANNING

Take the quiz about special events. Go to Follow A Pro on page 136 to find the answers. Then learn more about the event planning industry.

1 Social media is the best way to tell people about an event.
a true **b** false

2 How many weddings are there in the US every year?
a 1.2 million **b** 2.4 million **c** 158,000

3 How many birthday cards do people send every year?
a one million **b** one billion **c** two billion

4 40% of couples spend … hours per week planning their wedding.
a 1–5 **b** 5–10 **c** 10–15

UNIT 11 Planning Ahead

WHAT DO YOU ALREADY KNOW?

1 Think of words you know about present and future goals. Write the words.

2 IN PAIRS Share and compare your information. Add more words to your lists.

Present

Future

VIDEO

DISCUSS & SHARE

3 IN GROUPS Watch the video and answer the question.

SYM Do you think of your future or live for now?

In this unit, you will ...

- talk about plans and intentions, ways to save money, and your career goals.
- use thinking skills: apply, calculate, and analyze.
- read about making to-do lists.
- use strategies to keep talking by suggesting alternatives.
- use self-direction skills to make a career plan based on your interests.
- learn tips about personal development.

READING

A Which statement is true for you? Check (✓) and explain.

I use to-do lists every day. I need them to organize my time! ☐
I sometimes use to-do lists when I have a lot of things to remember. ☐
I never use to-do lists. I keep it all in my head! ☐

B 11.01 Read the article and discuss the question.

1 What mistake do people make with to-do lists?

WHAT TO DO ABOUT TO-DO LISTS

What are you going to do today?

Maybe you're going to write an important email, shop for a gift, or make a dentist **appointment**. We all have busy lives and it's easy to **forget** things we're supposed to do.

A list of things to do—or a "to-do list"—helps us **remember** what to do, but many people make a big mistake when they write their lists: they list a lot of things and then only do half of them. Here are some tips for writing a useful to-do list.

1 Write three things you are going to do in one day. Choose the things that are really important and write your list the night before. That way, you're **ready** to go in the morning!

2 When you have more than three things to do, write the top three and do them first. Then make a new list and write another three things. If you have one big job to do, break it into smaller jobs.

3 Write exactly what you need to do. Don't write "learn English." Write "learn eight new English words." People do things on their lists when it's **clear** what to do.

4 Be ready to change your list. Things are going to happen that you didn't **plan**. When they do, write a new list. Life is full of surprises!

C READING SKILL—Read for the main idea Choose the main idea of the text.

1 We should use to-do lists more.
2 To-do lists can be very helpful if you follow some basic tips.

D THINKING SKILL—Apply Write your to-do list for tomorrow. Follow the advice in the text. Compare lists with a partner.

VOCABULARY

A Complete with the words from the box.

appointment	clear	forget	plan	ready	remember

1 I have my phone and my money. I'm ______________ to go!
2 Things on your list should be ______________ and easy to understand.
3 I have a/an ______________ to see the doctor on Monday.
4 When you ______________ something on your list, you don't do it.
5 Did you ______________ to call your mom?
6 I ______________ to go shopping with friends on Saturday.

GRAMMAR *going to*

A Underline the sentences with *going to* in the article from READING B.

B Read the sentences you underlined. Complete the rule.

1 Before *going to*, we use the verb ________ in the correct form.
a *be* b *have* c *do*

2 After *going to*, we use the ________ of the verb.
a base form b *–ing* form c infinitive

3 We use *going to* to talk about plans and ________.
a offers b requests c predictions

For more practice, go to page 157.

C Read and complete the plans (1–2) and predictions (3–4).

1 A: What are you going to do this weekend?
B: Oh, ________________________________! (see my cousins)

2 A: Do you and your friend have any plans for tonight?
B: Yes! ________________________________. (go dancing)

3 A: What do you think about your exams?
B: I'm really worried. I think ________________________________! (fail)

4 A: It's a beautiful day!
B: Yeah … but ________________________________. (get cold later)

D IN PAIRS Discuss the questions.

1 What are you going to do tonight? What else is going to happen then?
2 What are you going to do this weekend? What else is going to happen then?

PRONUNCIATION *going to*

A 11.02 Listen and notice how the speakers say *going to*. *Going to* is often pronounced /gʌnə/. Practice saying the dialogues in GRAMMAR C.

SPEAKING

A Do you agree or disagree with the predictions? Then add your own prediction.

	Strongly agree	Agree	Not sure	Disagree	Strongly disagree
1 More education is going to help me get a job.	☐	☐	☐	☐	☐
2 I'm going to own a successful business before I'm 30.	☐	☐	☐	☐	☐
3 My career is going to change a lot in the next five years.	☐	☐	☐	☐	☐
4 ________________________________	☐	☐	☐	☐	☐

B Choose a statement you agree with in A. Write a plan to help your prediction come true.

I'm going to own a successful business before I'm 30. I'm going to start my own online business ...

C IN PAIRS Talk about your predictions and plans. Use the Confident Communicator box to help you.

CONFIDENT COMMUNICATOR
START TALKING

To ask about future plans, say: *What are you going to do?* To ask about future plans at a specific time in the future, say: *What are you going to do* + time expression, e.g., *What are you going to do tomorrow / next month / in December?*

LESSON 2 Saving for the Future

VOCABULARY money

A Match the opposites. Write the number (1–6).

buy ____

spend ____

sell ____

rich ____

save ____

poor ____

B IN PAIRS Discuss the questions.

1 Do you save money every month or do you spend all of it?
2 What was the last thing you bought? What was the last thing you sold?

LISTENING

A Look at the picture. What do you think the person in the picture is doing? Why is he doing that?

B 11.03 LISTENING SKILL—Listen for specific information
Listen and match each person (1–2) to the reason why they want to save money (a–b). Write the letter.

1 David ____	a to rent an apartment
2 Patricia ____	b to go on vacation

C 11.03 Listen again and choose *True* or *False*.

1 David earns a lot from his job.	True / False
2 He spends a lot of money on rent.	True / False
3 He is going to save money on food.	True / False
4 Patricia wants to spend money on expensive gifts.	True / False
5 She made a photo album for her mom.	True / False
6 She wants her brother to make her a pizza.	True / False

D THINKING SKILL—Calculate Estimate how much you can save doing what David and Patricia are going to do.

MAKE IT YOURS

Make a list of things you spent money on this month. Then make a list of ways you could save money next month.

GRAMMAR direct and indirect objects

A Read and complete the rules.

David: This month, I'm going to make sandwiches for myself.
Patricia: I'm going to make him pizza!

1 In "make sandwiches for myself," *sandwiches* is the direct object. What is the indirect object? ____________

2 In "make him pizza," *pizza* is the direct object. What is the indirect object? ____________

Some verbs can take a direct object and an indirect object. Notice the word order.

3 subject + verb + direct object + preposition + indirect object
People give gifts ____________ *each other.*

4 subject + verb + indirect object + direct object
People give each other ____________.

5 Use the preposition ____________ with the verbs *give, bring, sell, send, show,* and *tell.*

6 Use the preposition *for* with the verbs *buy, cook,* and *make.*

For more practice, go to page 157.

B Rewrite the underlined phrases. Do not use a preposition.

Money-saving tips

Why don't you make a gift for your friend for her birthday?

1 ____

You could cook a meal for your family and save on eating out.

2 ____

You could buy local food for a visitor as a souvenir of his visit.

3 ____

When your friends have a party, why not bring homemade cookies for them?

4 ____

C IN PAIRS Write two more money-saving tips in your notebook. Use two of the verbs from A.

SPEAKING

A Make a list of reasons for saving money in your notebook.

B Role-play a conversation. Student A, you want to save money for a nice birthday gift for a family member. Tell your partner why you want to save money and ask him or her how to save money. Student B, suggest ways Student A could save money. Use the Confident Communicator box to help you.

CONFIDENT COMMUNICATOR
KEEP TALKING

To suggest alternatives, use *You could …* e.g., *You could make lunch at home.* You can also use negative questions with *Why don't you …?* e.g., *Why don't you make a gift?*

Career Plans

VOCABULARY career plans collocations

A Check (✓) the things you want to do in your future career.

1

work outdoors

2

manage people

3

work in an office

4

start a business

5

work from home

6

work overseas

B IN PAIRS Discuss your future career plans. Use phrases from A.

I want to work for a large company. I'm probably going to manage other people. I also want to work overseas …

LISTENING

A IN PAIRS What do you need to do to get your dream job? Discuss.

B 11.04 LISTENING SKILL—Listen for gist Listen and make notes on Jade's advice.

How to get your dream job:

First, ______________________________

____

Second, ______________________________

____

Finally, ______________________________

____

C THINKING SKILL—Analyze Decide what other advice is useful for getting your dream job.

- Talk to people with the job you want.
- Network with family and friends.
- Volunteer at places with similar jobs.
- Go to job fairs.
- other: ______________________________

WRITING

A Read the journal entry. Underline sentences with *so* and *because*.

Saturday, May 15

It's time to think about my career, so I need to set some goals and make a plan. In the next two years, I'm going to start my own business because I want to be the boss. I know a lot about cooking, so I want to open my own restaurant!

I need to learn more about cooking and food safety, so I'm going to study at a culinary college that teaches those things. Then, I'm going to take a business course. I have to understand money and business to run a restaurant.

And finally, I'm going to practice cooking because I need to improve my skills!

Well, that's my plan!

FOLLOW

B Choose the correct phrases to complete the rules.

1 Use *so* to talk about the result of / reason for something.
2 Use *because* to explain the result of / reason for something.

C Complete the career plan with your own goals.

In my future career, I'm going to ________________________________

So, I'm going to ________________________________

____

because ________________________________

____

D Write a journal entry describing your career plans in your notebook.

SPEAKING

A Make notes to answer the questions.

1 What is your dream job? ________________________________
2 What are you going to do to get that job?
learn a skill | do an internship | get a degree/certificate

____

3 Do you think you will use English in your dream job? How?

____

B IN PAIRS Discuss your career plans and if English is important for your dream job. Use the Confident Communicator box to help you.

CONFIDENT COMMUNICATOR
REPAIR IT

When you aren't sure about what you are saying, at the start of your sentence, say: *I guess* or *I suppose*.
I guess I'm going to use English with people on the phone.

Language and Life

Self-direction – From Hobby to Career

A 11.05 **Read the article. Answer the questions.**

Follow Your Passion

15. Oct 11:24

Many of us have a hobby or a free-time activity we love, but is it possible to make that hobby a career? For some people, the answer is "yes." Love baking? Start a cake-making business. Exercise every day? Start a career as a personal trainer. Today, lots of people are finding that social media can help them turn their passion into a career.

Fiorella Pia has an interesting hobby. She takes photographs of food and shares them on a social networking website. She has a talent for making the food look nice. She has a lot of followers and her pictures are very popular. Now she wants to turn her hobby into a career. She wants to earn money from her photography. She's going to plan carefully. She needs to decide exactly what kind of business to start. She also needs to write a business plan. She's asking all her friends for their advice as she puts together her career plan.

Read more

1 Which hobbies can become careers, according to the article? __________

2 What is Fiorella's hobby? __________

3 What does she want to do now? __________

B **IN GROUPS Make a list of careers that involve photography. Then compare your lists as a class. Which group thought of the most careers?**

wedding photographer

photojournalist

____

____

C Read the information. Then decide what Fiorella's A/B/Z choices should be.

When you are making a career plan, it's a good idea to have "A/B/Z" choices. Reid Hoffman, founder of LinkedIn, created the A/B/Z plan. An "A" choice is your dream choice. This is the career you really want. You need a bit of luck to get it, but this is your dream career.

Your "B" choice is your alternative plan. This is the choice for when Plan A doesn't work out. It isn't your dream career, but it is close.

Your "Z" choice is an emergency choice. This is what you can do when Plan A and Plan B don't succeed. Perhaps you can do this for a short time and think about a new Plan A/B.

Fiorella Pia's Career Plan:

1 A choice: ______________________________

2 B choice: ______________________________

3 Z choice: ______________________________

D IN GROUPS Discuss the different goals Fiorella should have. Make a list of clear short-term, mid-term, and long-term goals.

Short-term goals (up to 1 year):

do 3 or 4 weddings as a photographer and build a website

____

____

Mid-term goals (1–5 years):

employ one assistant and rent a studio

____

____

Long-term goals (5 years +):

employ photographers and open studios in three major cities

____

____

E IN PAIRS Ask and answer questions about your choices and suggestions.

1 Explain your A/B/Z choices for Fiorella.
2 Say what you think her short-, mid-, and long-term goals should be.

F IN PAIRS Discuss the questions.

1 Do you have a hobby that could become a career?
2 What could you do to make money from your hobby?
3 Is it always a good idea to make a career out of a hobby? Are there any possible problems?

MAKE IT DIGITAL

Go online and find careers related to your favorite hobby. Make a list of your A/B/Z choices.

VOCABULARY review

SCORE: / 10

A Complete the conversation with words from the box.

appointment business luck manage overseas ready remember saved sell skills

Nate: Excuse me. Ms. King? I'm Nate West. We have a 2:30 **1** ____________.
Ms. King: Of course, I **2** ____________. Have a seat. So, tell me about yourself, Nate.
Nate: Well, right now I work part-time in a café. I'm good with money and **3** ____________ people well. I think these are good **4** ____________. I **5** ____________ some money from my job, so after I graduate, I plan to work **6** ____________ for a year, maybe in Colombia.
Ms. King: Why is that?
Nate: You see, I'd like to start a **7** ____________ someday. I want to **8** ____________ coffee to cafés. But I'm not **9** ____________ to do that now. First, I need to learn about growing coffee. I think with a little **10** ____________, it can be a big success.

GRAMMAR review

SCORE: / 10

A Complete the sentences with the correct form of *be going to* and the verb in parentheses.

1 Greg and Lisa ____________________ (get) married on Sunday.
2 My brother is sick, so he ____________________ (not go) to work today.
3 ____________________ you ____________________ (visit) me this weekend?
4 Where ____________________ your sister ____________________ (go) after work?
5 My mother and father ____________________ (spend) the weekend with me.

B Choose the correct option.

1 Ken and Zoe's wedding is this weekend. Let's buy a special gift for him / it / them.
2 Mr. Green doesn't feel well. Why don't we make us / him / it some chicken soup?
3 Can you give it / me / you a campus tour? I'm new here.
4 Mrs. Ortega's company wants to send it / her / she to Moscow for three weeks.
5 Your parents are in town? Do you plan to cook dinner for him / her / them?

16–20 correct: You can talk about to-do lists, money, and career plans. You can use *going to*, direct and indirect objects.
0–15 correct: Look again at the Vocabulary and Grammar sections in the unit.

TOTAL SCORE: / 20

WHAT DO YOU KNOW NOW? Look back at page 107 and add the words you know now to the boxes.

STUDY SKILLS PERSONAL DEVELOPMENT

Take the quiz about time management. Go to **Study Skills** on page 137 to find the answers. Then learn more about time management.

1 **... of business and professional people regularly write to-do lists.**
a 20% **b** 40% **c** 70%

2 **Around ... of students feel stressed every day.**
a 49% **b** 68% **c** 99%

3 **The average person uses ... different methods to manage their time.**
a 3 **b** 7 **c** 13

4 **Students who do their work at the last minute get ... students who finish their work early.**
a better grades than **b** worse grades than **c** the same grades as

UNIT 12

The Great Outdoors

WHAT DO YOU ALREADY KNOW?

1 **Think of words you know about the weather, climate, seasons, and natural features where you live. Write the words.**

2 **IN PAIRS** **Share and compare your words. Add more words to your lists.**

Weather / Climate

Seasons

Natural features

DISCUSS & SHARE

VIDEO

3 **IN GROUPS** **Watch the video and answer the question.**

SYM Are you an adventurer?

In this unit, you will ...

- talk about climate, weather, natural features, and outdoor activities.
- use thinking skills: infer, hypothesize, and recall.
- read about the Galapagos Islands.
- use strategies to keep talking by showing interest.
- use problem-solving skills to decide how to develop a natural area.
- read about a forest ranger to learn about this job and the skills needed for the environmental field.

LESSON 1 Different Climates

READING

A Look at the pictures in the brochure in B. Answer the questions.

1 What are the people in the photographs doing?
2 Do you enjoy these kinds of activities?

B 12.01 Read the brochure. Answer the questions.

The Galapagos **Islands** are an amazing place for a tour. There are beautiful sandy beaches, awesome animals, and the people are friendly. Every year, new people learn what the Galapagos Islands have to offer. People can swim, dive, and see nature—the Galapagos have it all!

The islands are near the **equator.** They don't have seasons like some other places do, but there is a **cool** season from June to November. The water is colder at that time, and there's less rain, so it's drier. It's a great time for diving around the islands. It's also a good time to see whales, sea lions, and penguins. The **temperature** is around 21–27°C, and the water is around 18–24°C.

From December to May, the temperature is higher. It's called the warm season. It's more **tropical** during these months, and the skies are cloudier. It's also wetter than the rest of the year. The ocean is warmer and it's better for swimming. It's also a good time to see iguanas, flamingos, and other tropical birds. The temperature is around 27–32°C. The water is cooler than that, at around 21–26°C.

To get there, you need to go to Ecuador. From Ecuador, you can fly to Baltra Island or San Cristóbal Island, or go by boat. Of course, it's quicker to fly than go by boat. Flights are also cheaper, but then you have to pay for a hotel. A luxury cruise ship is more expensive than a trip on a small boat.

1 What time of year is better for diving in the Galapagos Islands?
2 What time of year is better for swimming?
3 How can you get to the Galapagos Islands?

MAKE IT REAL

Most countries use the Celsius scale to measure temperature. For 27–32°C, we say "twenty-seven to thirty-two degrees Celsius." A few countries, including the United States, use Fahrenheit (F).

C READING SKILL—Scan for specific information Read and complete.

1 What is the air temperature in April? ______________
2 Is it wet or dry in September? ______________
3 When is the water temperature 18–24°C? ______________
4 When is a good time for seeing flamingos? ______________

D THINKING SKILL—Understand Answer the questions.

1 What time of year is there more rain in the Galapagos Islands?
2 Why don't the Galapagos Islands have spring, summer, fall, and winter?

VOCABULARY

A Complete with words and phrases from READING B.

1 These are areas of land that have water around them. ______________
2 This is an imaginary line around the center of the Earth. ______________
3 This describes weather that is not very hot, or a little cold. ______________
4 This tells you how hot or cold a place is. ______________
5 This describes weather that is very hot and wet. ______________

GRAMMAR comparative adjectives

A Read the text in READING B again. Underline the comparatives.

The water is colder and there is less rain, so it's drier.

B Complete the table with the examples.

Most one-syllable adjectives	Add *–er*: *long–longer, cold–* **1** ________, *quick–* **2** ________
One-syllable adjectives ending in *–e*	Add *–r*: *nice–nicer, rare–rarer*
One–syllable adjectives ending in consonant–vowel–consonant	Double the final consonant and add *–er*: *hot–hotter, wet–* **3** ________
One- or two-syllable adjectives ending in *–y*	Change the *y* to *i* and add *–er*: *dry–* **4** ________, *happy–happier*
Adjectives with two or more syllables	Use *more* or *less*: *interesting–more/less interesting, expensive–* **5** ________
Irregular adjectives	*bad–worse, good–* **6** ________

When comparing two things directly in the same sentence, use *than*: *Today is hotter than yesterday.*

For more practice, go to page 158.

C Complete the text using the comparative form of the words given. Add *than* if needed.

Peru has three different regions: the coast, the Andes, and the rain forest. They all have different climates. The coast is **1** ________ (cool) the other two regions, with average temperatures of 18°C in Lima in August. The weather is **2** ________ (warm) in February, with average temperatures of 27°C.

In the Andes, the weather is **3** ________ (wet) from September to May, and **4** ________ (dry) from June to August. The Andes is **5** ________ (sunny) the coastal area.

The rain forest is **6** ________ (rainy) the coast and the Andes. It is also **7** ________ (hot), with average temperatures of 30–32°C all year round.

SPEAKING

A Research the climate of a country or city you are interested in. Write down the temperature and weather at different times of the year.

B IN PAIRS Student A, you want to visit your friend. Ask about the weather in your friend's country or city at different times of the year. Student B, tell your friend about the weather in your country or city at different times of the year. Then change roles. Decide where you both would like to go on a trip, and when. Use your notes and the Confident Communicator box to help you.

CONFIDENT COMMUNICATOR

KEEP TALKING

To learn about a place, say: *What's it like?*
To ask about weather, say: *What's it like in summer?* or *What's it like in February?*

LESSON 2 Natural Features

VOCABULARY natural features

A **Check (✓) the natural features you can find less than 100 kilometers (60 miles) from where you live.**

desert

forest

hill

lake

mountain

river

volcano

waterfall

B **IN PAIRS** **Name examples of each natural feature in your country.**

An example of a waterfall here in Chile is the Laja Falls.

LISTENING

A **Look at the picture. Where do you think this place is?**

MAKE IT YOURS

Can you think of more natural features in your country? Find out what they are called.

B **12.02 Listen and choose *True* or *False*.**

1 Kerry is a student. True / False
2 The Iguazu River starts in Argentina. True / False
3 Niagara Falls is just one waterfall. True / False
4 The speaker went to Angel Falls last year. True / False

C **12.02 LISTENING SKILL—Listen for specific information** **Listen again and complete the table.**

	Country	Height	Number of waterfalls	Good time to visit
Iguazu Falls			300	
Niagara Falls	Canada/US	50 meters		
Angel Falls				May–October

D **THINKING SKILL—Induce** **Answer the questions.**

1 Which of the waterfalls do you want to see? Why?
2 How do you think people feel when they visit places like Iguazu Falls?

GRAMMAR review of tenses

A Match the sentences. Write the letters.

1 I love waterfalls because **I'm studying** geology in college and waterfalls are great places to learn more. ____
2 When it gets to the border with Argentina, **it falls** 82 meters. ____
3 Last year, **I went** to the Iguazu Falls in Argentina and Brazil. ____
4 **I'm going to visit** Angel Falls next May because the water is higher then. ____

a This is a single action in the past.
b This is a future plan.
c This is true in the present.
d This is generally true.

For more practice, go to page 159.

B Complete with the correct form of the verbs from the box.

feel go (×2) have learn love stay

Two months ago, I **1** ____________ to the White Mountain National Forest in Maine. The forest **2** ____________ many hiking trails and lakes. I **3** ____________ there for a week and camped. It **4** ____________ great to be outdoors, under the stars at night. I **5** ____________ how to catch fish right now. Next time I go to Maine, I **6** ____________ swimming in the lakes. Nature is very important to me. I **7** ____________ the outdoors!

C Play a game of *True or False?* Write two things that are true about you and one thing that is false. Use the time expressions. Ask your partner to guess if your statements are true or false. Take turns.

Last year, I … *Right now, I …* *Next month, I …*

Last year, I flew on a plane. Right now, I'm learning the piano. Next month, I'm going to visit my cousin in the US.

SPEAKING

A Think of a natural place you enjoyed visiting. Make notes on what you know or what you want to find out about it.

Place: ______________________________

Facts: ______________________________

____

B Make notes on what happened when you went there. How did you feel there?

____

____

C IN PAIRS Discuss. Tell your partner about the place you visited. Use your notes from A and B. Use the Confident Communicator box to help you.

CONFIDENT COMMUNICATOR
KEEP TALKING

When someone tells a story, we can respond using the phrases:
That's very interesting!
That sounds really good/bad.
How interesting/wonderful/sad!

LESSON 3 Wonders of the Natural World

VOCABULARY adjectives to describe natural features

A Circle the positive adjectives and underline the negative adjectives.

amazing attractive awesome beautiful boring fantastic popular ugly

B Choose three places. Say what you know and think about them. Explain.

I think the Grand Canyon is awesome! It's beautiful and I want to see it one day.

THE SEVEN NATURAL WONDERS OF THE WORLD

Mount Everest, Himalayas, China/Nepal

Grand Canyon, Arizona, US

Great Barrier Reef, Australia

Parícutin Volcano, Mexico

Aurora Borealis, near the Arctic

Harbor of Rio de Janeiro, Brazil

Victoria Falls, Zambia/Zimbabwe

PRONUNCIATION /ju/

A 12.03 Listen and notice. The long *u* sound /u/ sometimes has a *y* sound /ju/.

beautiful communicate cute document music popular

B Practice saying the words with the correct pronunciation.

LISTENING

A 12.04 Look at the phrases and guess the natural wonder. Then listen to check.

… it appeared in a corn field …

… it grew very quickly …

… local people take visitors …

… on horseback …

B 12.04 LISTENING SKILL—Listen for detail Listen and answer the questions.

1 When did it appear? ______________
2 How can you get to the small town near the volcano? by ______________ or ______________
3 How can you get to the volcano from the town? ______________
4 How can you get to the top of the volcano? ______________
5 How long is the complete trip? ______________

C THINKING SKILL—Recall Tell a partner what you learned about the volcano. Do you want to visit the volcano? Why or why not?

WRITING

A Read the guidebook entry and check (✓) the information the writer mentions.

HAKONE, JAPAN, is a town with many hot springs. Hot springs are places with natural hot water that comes up from the ground. The Hakone hot springs are very popular with local people and tourists. You can relax in the hot water and enjoy the amazing natural views. Hakone is about 90 minutes from Tokyo by train. It is close to the famous Mount Fuji. You can take a train to Odawara Station and then take a bus. Hakone is 20 minutes by bus from the train station. There are many hotels in Hakone if you want to stay for a few days. You can also go on a tour of the area. Search "Hakone hot springs" online for more information.

- who enjoys this place ☐
- what you can do here ☐
- where it is ☐
- how to get there ☐
- how much the train costs ☐
- where to stay ☐
- where to learn more ☐

B Choose a local natural feature you know. Answer the questions.

1 What place are you going to write about? ____________________
2 Why is it interesting or attractive? ____________________
3 What can you do there? ____________________
4 Where is it? How can you get there? ____________________
5 Can you stay there? Where? ____________________
6 Is there a website with more information? ____________________

C Write a guidebook entry for young adults from other countries. Use your answers in B to create your entry.

SPEAKING

A Choose an outdoor activity to talk about. Make notes to answer the questions.

1 Where can you do this activity in your area?

____

2 What do you like about this activity?

____

3 Is there anything you dislike about this activity?

____

MAKE IT YOURS

Some guidebooks ask people to write about their local area for tourists. Do you know any examples of guidebooks like that? What do you think is interesting about guidebook writing?

B IN PAIRS Talk about the outdoor activities in A. Use the Confident Communicator box to help you.

CONFIDENT COMMUNICATOR

KEEP TALKING

When you are listing points (e.g., things you like about an activity), you can use *One thing I like about it is …* and *Another thing I like about it is …*

***One thing I like about camping** is that you sleep under the stars!*
***Another thing I like about it is** it's really quiet at night.*

Language and Life

Problem-solving – Developing a Natural Area

A 12.05 **Read the newspaper article. Answer the questions.**

LOCAL COLLEGE ASKS FOR IDEAS

by Janice Baskin

Meadowville College is a college near our city. There is a large lake and a forest on Meadowville's campus. Right now, not many people use the lake or the forest. Some people go swimming or camping there in the summer.

Recently, the college decided to use this area for its students. Dean Linda Collins says, "We want our students to learn about nature and learn new skills. Many of our students come from big cities and they don't know a lot about nature. They are more familiar with technology than they are with the natural world." The college wants students to be interested in nature. "They need activities to introduce them to outdoor life. Maybe something that uses technology can get them interested—something that connects nature to their studies," says Dean Collins.

The college is asking students for ideas and suggestions. They have money for the project and they are happy to spend it on the right ideas.

1 Where are the lake and the forest? ______
2 What do people do there right now? ______
3 What does the college want students to learn? ______
4 Why don't some students know much about nature? ______
5 What does the college want from students? ______

B **IN GROUPS** **Read the statements from students. Talk about the ideas and check (✓) the ones you think are good suggestions.**

1 What about an app with useful information about the natural features on campus? ☐
2 They should buy boats and tents and leave us to explore the area on our own. ☐
3 We need an information center where we can learn about the natural history. ☐
4 They should get instructors to teach courses on swimming and camping. ☐
5 Other: ______ ☐

C IN PAIRS Choose one of the ideas. Answer the questions.

☐ **Relaxation**
They should make quiet, relaxing areas where students can chat and study on their own.

☐ **Sports**
They should build a sports center and have instructors offer classes for different outdoor sports or activities.

☐ **Technology**
They should create a mobile app that gives useful information to get people interested in exploring the area.

☐ **Nature**
They should build a center where students can learn about the wildlife and history of the area.

1 What are the main points that support your idea?

____

____

____

2 What is the main point against your idea?

____

____

____

3 What do you say to argue that point?

____

____

____

D Take turns. Explain your ideas to the class. Give reasons.

We think the college should build a nature center. It can even have art classes, so students can paint pictures of nature. Also, …

E Take a vote with your class. Choose the idea you like best. Don't vote for your own idea.

MAKE IT DIGITAL

You are going to post your idea on the college website. What information should you give about your idea? What images should you use?

VOCABULARY review

SCORE: / 10

A Choose the correct option.

There are many boats on the **1 desert / river**. Boat tours are very **2 ugly / popular**.
People left cans and bottles at the top of the **3 mountain / forest**. **4** It was **ugly / awesome**.
The **5 island / volcano** looked red and orange at night. The colors were **6 beautiful / boring**.
I walked in the **7 forest / waterfall** all day. I had so much fun. It was **8 amazing / boring**.
I swam in a lake under the **9 forest / waterfall**. It was **10 fantastic / attractive**!

GRAMMAR review

SCORE: / 10

A Read the information. Then complete the sentences with the comparative form of a word in the box. Add *than*.

expensive high long hot wet

The Mississippi River: 3,734 m / The Mekong River: 4,350 m
Yearly rainfall in Chicago: 93 cm / Yearly rainfall in Boston: 111 cm
Hotels in Istanbul: \$120–\$130 / Hotels in Panama City: \$130–\$140
Mt. Blanc: 4,808 m / Mt. Fuji: 3,776 m
Miami: 32°C / Montreal: 24°C

1 The Mekong River is ______________________.
2 Boston is ______________________.
3 Hotels in Panama City are ______________________.
4 Mt. Blanc is ______________________.
5 Miami is ______________________.

B Complete the paragraph with the correct form of the verb in parentheses.

Every year my friend Wendy and I **1** ____________ (take) a two-week vacation. We're in Belize right now. The sun **2** ____________ (shine) and we're on a beautiful beach. I **3** ____________ (learn) how to scuba dive now. Tomorrow we **4** ____________ (dive) in the famous Blue Hole. I **5** ____________ (learn) about this in one of my classes last year.

16–20 correct: You can talk about natural features and adjectives to describe them. You can use comparative adjectives.
0–15 correct: Look again at the Vocabulary and Grammar sections in the unit.

TOTAL SCORE: / 20

WHAT DO YOU KNOW NOW? Look back at page 117 and add the words you know now to the boxes.

FOLLOW A PRO NATURAL SCIENCE

Take the quiz about careers in natural science. Go to **Follow A Pro** on page 138 to find the answers. Then learn more about careers in natural science.

1 How many gardeners and florists say they are happy in their job?
a 52% **b** 79% **c** 87%

2 Spending … outside gives your brain as much energy as drinking one cup of coffee.
a 10 minutes **b** 20 minutes **c** 1 hour

3 Nearly half of all jobs need some kind of outdoor work.
a true **b** false

4 One park ranger, Roy Sullivan, lived through seven lightning strikes and … bear encounters in his 40-year career.
a 22 **b** 7 **c** 13

UNIT 1

STUDY SKILLS

A **Read about memory strategies. People remember new information in different ways. Which way is best for you?**

MEMORY STRATEGIES

Ricardo I use different colors to take notes in my notebook because it helps me learn. Nouns are in red, verbs are in green, and adjectives are in yellow.

Maya I love art, and I make pictures with new words and phrases. After that, I don't forget them!

Sol I learn words that go together. So, I write down family words together, words for colors together, and words for jobs together.

Meera When I learn a new word, I write it down 10 times. That helps me to remember it!

Ana I make a sentence that's true for me with the new word. So, if I learn the word *swim*, then my sentence is "I swim every Saturday," because that's true for me.

Bob I talk about my learning with my friends and tell them the new words I know. I don't like learning things alone!

B **Match the example (1–6) to the memory strategy (a–f). Write the letter.**

a writing new words 10 times
b sharing learning with friends
c making sentences with new words
d using different colors
e making pictures to learn things
f learning words that go together

1 *player play playful* ______

2 *hand*  ______

3 *mother, father, sister, brother, aunt, uncle* ______

4 *beautiful, beautiful, beautiful, beautiful, beautiful, beautiful, beautiful, beautiful, beautiful, beautiful* ______

5 *I study in the library. I don't study on Sundays.* ______

6  ______

C **Complete the sentences with the words from the box.**

laugh stories listen

1 I record my voice saying new words. Then, I ______________.
2 I put new words together to make ______________. That helps me remember.
3 I make a funny joke out of new words. If I ______________, I remember!

MAKE IT HAPPEN

Choose 10 new words you want to learn. Use three of the memory strategies to help you learn them. With a partner, talk about the three memory strategies. Use the phrases to help you.

A: I think that it's a good idea to study with friends.

B: I agree. And I want to use colors for my notes. It's easy to remember the new words that way.

D **IN PAIRS Discuss the memory strategies you want to use. Use B and C to help you.**

A: I want to sing the new words I learn because I love music.

B: That's a good idea. I don't like singing, so I want to make stories from the new words I learn.

E **THINKING SKILL—Remember Observe what kind of memory you have.**

1 Do you have a good memory for some things and not others?
2 What are some things that are difficult to memorize?
3 When do you need a good memory at your job?

Answers to the quiz on page 16
1 a 2 b 3 a 4 c

UNIT 2

FOLLOW A PRO

A Read about an IT consultant's job. Answer the questions below.

AN IT CONSULTANT

My name is Tim Watkins. I'm an IT consultant at my family's company, IT Computer Consultants. Our office is in the city center, not too far from my apartment. I help people with their computer problems. My sister is an accountant. She works with the company accounts. Her husband, Bob, is a computer technician. He has a degree in computer engineering. My mom is creative, and she likes to write. She's the social media marketing manager. She manages our website, writes our blog, and posts on social media. My dad is friendly and organized. He's the general manager. It's a good business and it does really well. I like working with my family.

1 Whose business is IT Computer Consultants? ____________________
2 What does Tim help people with? ____________________
3 Who is Bob? ____________________
4 Why is Tim's mom the social media marketing manager? ____________________
5 What does Tim's dad do? ____________________

B Discuss the questions as a class.

1 Is a family business a good idea? Why or why not?
2 Can you imagine your own family business?

VIDEO

WATCH THE VIDEO AND FOLLOW AN IT PROFESSIONAL.

C IN GROUPS Answer the questions.

1 What job is the video about? ____________________
2 Who does the job? ____________________
3 What special skills or education does this person have? ____________________
4 Does this person like the job? ____________________
5 What are some of the good and bad things about the job? ____________________
6 How does this person use English at work? ____________________

D IN GROUPS Check your answers to the quiz on page 26 and discuss the questions.

1 Do you know people who work in IT?
2 What other IT jobs do you know?
3 Do you want this kind of job? Why or why not?
4 Is there an opportunity to have this kind of job where you live?
5 What skills does an IT professional need?

Answers to the quiz on page 26
1 a 2 b 3 c 4 c

STUDY SKILLS

A Read the oral presentations. Which presentation do you think is better and why?

ORAL PRESENTATIONS

1 Ella

The teacher says we have to do a talk, so … my talk is about photography. I do it every day and I like it. I don't know why. It's fun. I like it. My camera is good—it's a Lumix. And … um … I take pictures every day, and I also take pictures on weekends. My camera is black and it's not too big. And … this is my favorite picture. Um … yeah.

2 Vanessa

Hello, everyone. I want to talk to you today about my favorite hobby, swimming. I really enjoy swimming because it makes me feel good and it gives me energy. I swim every day at the swimming pool near my house. I also swim with the school swimming club: the Dolphins. There are 10 students in the club, and we swim in competitions with other schools. I love doing that! Our teacher is Mr. Skinner. He's a great swimming teacher. I like swimming because it's fun, it's good for me, and it doesn't cost a lot of money. Thank you for listening! Any questions?

B Write *Ella* or *Vanessa* next to the sentence each person said.

1 ______________ says hello.
2 ______________ talks about a favorite hobby.
3 ______________ stops and starts when she gives her presentation.
4 ______________ explains why she likes her hobby.
5 ______________ organizes her presentation.
6 ______________ isn't sure what she is talking about.
7 ______________ doesn't finish in a clear way.

C Match the tips about oral presentations (1–6) to the explanations (a–f). Write the letter.

1 Smile and look at your listeners. _____
2 Don't speak fast. Take your time. _____
3 Plan your presentation. _____
4 Organize your presentation. Use words like *First*, *Second*, and *Next*. _____
5 Tell an interesting story. Don't just use facts and data. _____
6 Answer questions at the end of your presentation. _____

a People remember stories, but they forget facts and numbers.
b You feel nervous when you don't plan.
c Listeners need time to think as you speak.
d Your listeners feel comfortable when you are friendly.
e Your listeners can learn more when they ask questions.
f Present your ideas one at a time so your listeners can follow.

D Rewrite the first presentation in A as an interesting, clear presentation.

Hello, everyone. Welcome to my talk on photography …

E THINKING SKILL—Create Why is it a good idea to prepare and practice a presentation before you speak in public? In what jobs do you need oral presentation skills?

MAKE IT HAPPEN

Prepare an oral presentation on your favorite hobby. Organize your presentation with these questions.

When do you do your hobby?
Why do you like it?
Where do you do your hobby?
Who do you do your hobby with?

Answers to the quiz on page 36
1 b (You need to spend 70% of your time on writing.) 2 c 3 c 4 b

UNIT 4 FOLLOW A PRO

A Read about a firefighter's job. Answer the questions below.

A FIREFIGHTER

Sally Lane is a firefighter. She is at the fire station 24 hours a day for three days, and then she has three days off. On her workdays, Sally sleeps at the fire station. She gets up at 4:00 a.m., gets dressed, and eats breakfast with the other firefighters. She takes a shower in the evening, not in the morning. Sally usually works at least 15 hours on a workday. She fights fires, practices with the equipment, goes to the fire station gym, and takes online classes to learn new information about fighting fires. Sally's job is difficult, but she likes it. She says, "I love my job because the work is always exciting and interesting. I like to help people. It's not always easy. When we are busy, I don't have time to eat or sleep!"

1 Where does Sally sleep on workdays? ______
2 When does she get up on workdays? ______
3 Who does she eat breakfast with? ______
4 How many hours does Sally usually work? ______
5 What different things does she do at work? ______
6 Why does Sally like her job? ______

B Discuss the questions as a class.

1 Could you be a firefighter? Why or why not?
2 What are the good points and bad points about Sally's job?
3 There aren't many women firefighters. Why not?

VIDEO

WATCH THE VIDEO AND FOLLOW A PARAMEDIC.

C IN GROUPS Answer the questions.

1 What job is the video about? ______
2 What skills does the person need for the job? ______
3 Who does the person work with? ______
4 What's the most difficult part of the person's job? ______
5 Is the person happy in this job? ______
6 What is the person's work schedule? ______

D IN GROUPS Check your answers to the quiz on page 46 and discuss the questions.

1 Do you know any firefighters?
2 What other jobs in the emergency services do you know?
3 What are the good points and bad points of working in the emergency services?
4 What skills do you need to work in the emergency services?
5 What special physical abilities do you need to work in the emergency services?

Answers to the quiz on page 46
1 b 2 a 3 c 4 a

UNIT 5

STUDY SKILLS

A Read the texts. Who are the texts for?

RESEARCH SKILLS

Education at Morrison University

With an education major, you can study a subject you love and then teach others what you know! This major is a good choice for people who want to work with children or adults in school or college.

Courses include:

- Managing a class
- Health and well-being
- Art and creativity
- Teaching language

Good writing, math, and communication skills are necessary.

Students say:

"This major is fun! I loved it."

Prize for best education course in 1982.

99% of students at Morrison University get jobs after graduating.

Business at **Markston University**

Do you want to work in international business? With a business major, you can study how business, sales, and accounting work in different countries. Learn what you need to be successful.

Classes include:

- Marketing a product
- Growing a small business
- International business
- Social media today
- Accounting

You need math ability and a foreign language.

Students say: "This major prepares you for a life in business. I now have my own international hotel chain and it's doing very well."
—Sam Blackthorne, former student

95% of our graduates find jobs in business.

The university won "Best Business Major" in 2018.

B Write the letter *E* (Education) or *B* (Business) next to the sentences.

1. Students with this major find jobs in sales. _____
2. A student says the courses are fun. _____
3. You need to speak a foreign language to study this major. _____
4. This is a good major if you want to be a teacher. _____
5. You need good communication skills to study this major. _____

C Match the tips about research (1–5) to the reasons to do them (a–e). Write the letter.

1. Always check the date on the texts you read. _____
2. You don't always need to read every word. _____
3. Make sure the text you read was written by an expert. _____
4. Think critically about the information you find. _____
5. Write questions before you start researching. _____

a. You want the information to be correct.
b. You want to be sure that the information is up-to-date and not old.
c. Just look for the information you need—it's faster.
d. This helps you to focus on what to look for.
e. Don't believe everything you read. You have to use what you know to help you.

D Make a list of pros and cons about each of the majors in A. Share with your partner.

A: I think the education major looks good. Look! They won a prize, too.

B: Yes, but that was in 1982! I think the business major is better because …

E THINKING SKILL—Apply Do you often do research for your studies? Do you enjoy it? Why or why not? How do good research skills relate to jobs you know?

MAKE IT HAPPEN

Work with a partner. Look online and choose a major that interests you. Use the research tips in **C** to help you.

Answers to the quiz on page 56
1 a 2 b 3 b 4 b (It's 52.8%.)

UNIT 6

FOLLOW A PRO

A Read about a chief listening officer's job. Answer the questions below.

A CHIEF LISTENING OFFICER

What does a chief listening officer do? Dani Chavez, 29, the chief listening officer (CLO) for a soft drink company in the US, tells us about his job.

"I'm working on an idea for a new soft drink, and it's important that my company knows who buys our drinks—their age, nationality, hobbies, and so on. How do we do this? We "listen to" social media and find out what people are saying about our soft drinks. This helps us decide what products to make. Social media is very important in my job. When I see a negative comment about my company, I send that information to our Customer Service Center. They then try to understand why our customers are not happy.

Being a CLO is a new job, but there are already a lot of us. As for skills, it's very important that I have good listening skills."

1 Dani works for a …
   a social media company.
   b soft drink company.

2 "Listen to" in the text means to …
   a read what people are saying online.
   b hear what people are saying on the street.

3 What does Dani do when he sees a negative comment about his company?
   a He contacts the person who wrote it.
   b He sends the comment to the Customer Service Center.

4 A good CLO needs …
   a listening skills.   b creative skills.

B Discuss the questions as a class.

1 Do you think Dani's job is interesting? Why or why not?
2 What other skills (apart from listening skills) are important for this job?
3 How can Dani's work help his company to sell more soft drinks?

VIDEO

WATCH THE VIDEO AND FOLLOW A SOCIAL MEDIA MANAGER.

C IN GROUPS Answer the questions.

1 What job is the video about? ______
2 Does the person like the job? ______
3 Where does the person work? ______
4 What is the person's favorite part of the job? ______
5 What is difficult about the job? ______
6 What does this person do for the clients? ______

D IN GROUPS Check your answers to the quiz on page 66 and discuss the questions.

1 Do you know any people who work in marketing?
2 What other jobs in marketing do you know?
3 Do you need English for this job?
4 What skills do you need to work in marketing?
5 What personal qualities do you need to work in marketing?

Answers to the quiz on page 66
1 a 2 a 3 a 4 c

UNIT 7

STUDY SKILLS

A **Read the conversation. On a scale of 1–5, rate the group work (1 = no communication, 5 = excellent communication).**

EFFECTIVE GROUP WORK

Amy So, we don't have very much time to get our presentation on Australian culture ready. Are you listening, Marco?
Marco Um, yes—I'm just reading about Australian art …
Amy What artists do you want to talk about?
Marco I don't know yet. Sorry—I didn't read the book.
Amy Well, let's …
Tammi Hey, guys! Sorry I'm late! The traffic is bad today.
Amy Oh, that's okay. So, Marco—you're reading about Australian art. Can you talk about that for about two minutes? And can you talk about music, Tammi?
Tammi I'm not sure … I don't know very much about …
Marco And what are *you* doing for the presentation, Amy?
Amy Um … well, I don't know yet. I'm still thinking …
Marco Can you talk about food?
Amy No, I don't want to do that …
Tammi The sports teams?
Amy No, that's a terrible idea. What are you doing, Roberto? You're very quiet!
Tammi So, am I doing food, then?

B **Check (✓) the reasons the group is not working well together.**

- ☐ One student is late.
- ☐ One student wants to work alone.
- ☐ One student isn't well prepared.
- ☐ One student isn't saying anything.
- ☐ One student is negative about the other students' ideas.
- ☐ One student is talking on the phone to a friend.
- ☐ One student is giving jobs to other people but isn't doing any work.

C **Match the tips about group work (1–5) to the expressions (a–e). Write the letter.**

Tips

1. Include all members of the group. _____
2. Say when you agree with someone's idea. _____
3. Make suggestions. _____
4. Be positive about other people's ideas. _____
5. Share what you know. _____

Expressions

a Why don't we find some old pictures?
b Sara, what do you think?
c I think that's a really good idea!
d Yes, I agree with you.
e I read an interesting blog post about that …

D **Rewrite the conversation in A. Show how a group can work together well. Use the language in C to help you.**

Amy: What are we doing for our presentation?
Marco: I'm reading a book on Australian art. Can I do something about that?

E **THINKING SKILL—Understand Describe how teamwork is important in the workplace. What jobs need teamwork?**

✓ MAKE IT HAPPEN

Prepare a group presentation on a famous English-speaking person. Decide what to present and how to do the work. Remember to work as a team!

A: Let's do a presentation on Abraham Lincoln. He's an interesting man.
B: I have a good book about Abraham Lincoln.

Answers to the quiz on page 76
1 a 2 b 3 a 4 b

UNIT 8 FOLLOW A PRO

A Read about a food stylist's job. Answer the questions below.

A FOOD STYLIST

The photos of food in magazines, cookbooks, restaurant websites, and travel guides always look so good. Do you know why? It's because a food stylist works to make the food look amazing in pictures. And that's what I do. I'm Alfonso Garcia, and my job is to make food look real when it's not. For example, do you know that a bowl of strawberry ice cream isn't really ice cream? It's mashed potato! Ice cream melts very quickly in a hot studio, so we use pink mashed potato instead. And here's a disgusting idea—we put motor oil on meat to make it look delicious and hot! I love my job, but I can't eat the food I work with. It all goes in the trash can!

1 What does a food stylist do? ______
2 What do food stylists use instead of strawberry ice cream? Why? ______
______
3 Why do food stylists put motor oil on meat? ______
4 What happens to the food that Alfonso uses? ______

B Discuss the questions as a class.

1 How important is a food stylist's job?
2 Think about places where you see pictures of food. How does the food look?
3 Would you like to be a food stylist?

VIDEO

WATCH THE VIDEO AND FOLLOW A BAKER.

C IN GROUPS Answer the questions.

1 What job is the video about? ______
2 Where does the person work? ______
3 Is the person's job difficult? Why or why not? ______
4 What skills does the person need for the job? ______
5 Does the person work long hours? ______
6 What doesn't the person like about the job? ______
______

D IN GROUPS Check your answers to the quiz on page 86 and discuss the questions.

1 What different food industry jobs can you think of?
2 Which food industry job sounds most interesting to you?
3 What qualifications do you need to work in the food industry?
4 What skills and abilities do you need to work in the food industry?
5 What are the good and bad points about working in the food industry?

Answers to the quiz on page 86
1 a 2 a 3 a (to make it look fat)
4 b (They add the seeds by hand.)

STUDY SKILLS

A Read the two texts. Which one is formal and which one is informal? Why?

FORMAL VS. INFORMAL WRITING

Text 1

Corsica is an island on the south coast of France. The population is 330,000. The official language is French. Every year, more than three million people visit Corsica. Most people come in summer, when the weather is usually hot (the average temperature is 22°C, according to Météo France). It is warm and dry all year round.

In Corsica, you can swim in the sea and go to the beach. A lot of people go walking in the hills or visit the historical buildings. Sant'Antonino is a very old village in the northeast of Corsica. It goes back to the 9th century and is a popular place for tourists to visit.

Text 2

I love Corsica! I go to Corsica every year with my family and we always have a good time. It's a really cool place because it's so beautiful. The sea is very blue and the weather is always good—it never rains! The people are friendly, too, and there are lots of cafés and markets where you can find great fruit, cheese, and meat. Go there if you can!

B Write *Text 1* or *Text 2* for each sentence.

1 The writer uses sources with facts and data. ______________

2 The writer doesn't give a personal opinion. ______________

3 The writer says how he or she feels. ______________

4 The writer uses contractions (e.g., "it's" instead of "it is"). ______________

5 The writer groups ideas together in paragraphs. ______________

6 The writer uses an emoji. ______________

C Write whether the sentences are *Formal* or *Informal*.

1 Over 800 million people around the world do not have clean drinking water. ______________

2 I think that's so sad! ______________

3 It's a cool place to visit. ______________

4 First, we need to think about why this happens. ______________

5 I wanna try and answer that question. ______________

6 According to the *Daily Morning Times* news, hundreds of young people are going overseas to find work. ______________

D Rewrite the informal sentences in C so that they are formal and rewrite the formal sentences so that they are informal.

E THINKING SKILL—Analyze Compare and contrast when you have to write formally and when you can write informally. What happens if you write formally in an informal situation?

✓ MAKE IT HAPPEN

Write a formal paragraph about a country. Do some research online to find out facts about that country.

Panama is a country between Central and South America. It has a population of around four million. It is famous for the Panama Canal, which connects the Atlantic and Pacific Oceans.

Answers to the quiz on page 96

1 b 2 a 3 b 4 a

UNIT 10

FOLLOW A PRO

A Read about an event organizer. Answer the questions below.

AN EVENT ORGANIZER

Dale Langdon started Star Events, Inc. four years ago. He loves social events, and he likes to help people celebrate special times in their lives. It's not easy to organize a wedding for 300 people or an 80th birthday party for a large family, but Dale does that every day. Each event starts with a meeting. People tell Dale what kind of event they want and how many people they want to invite. Dale asks questions to find out more about the person's ideas. Dale then makes sure it all happens. He has to find a place for the event and make all preparations for the event—from the music to the parking. For some events, he has to find musicians, photographers, dancers, chefs, DJs, and servers. It's a lot of work, but Dale likes it.

1 Why did Dale start Star Events, Inc.? ______
2 What kind of events does Dale organize? ______
3 What does each event start with? ______
4 How does Dale find out what people want? ______
5 What services does Dale need to find? ______

B Discuss the questions as a class.

1 What do you think is enjoyable about this career?
2 What do you think is not enjoyable about this career?
3 Imagine you are an event organizer. A young woman wants an unusual event for her 21st birthday. Money isn't a problem. What do you suggest?

VIDEO

WATCH THE VIDEO AND FOLLOW A TOUR GUIDE.

C IN GROUPS Answer the questions.

1 Where does the person work? ______
2 What does the person do every day? ______
3 What does the person say is the best part of the job? ______
4 What skills does the person need? ______
5 Who does the person work with? ______

D IN GROUPS Check your answers to the quiz on page 106 and discuss the questions.

1 What different events do people need help with planning?
2 Which events take the most time and money to plan?
3 What personal qualities do you need to work in the events industry?
4 Are there opportunities for this job where you live?
5 Do you need English for this job?

Answers to the quiz on page 106
1 a 2 b 3 c 4 c

UNIT 11

STUDY SKILLS

A **Read the conversation. Is Maria a good time manager?**

PERSONAL DEVELOPMENT

Sally Hey, Maria! What are you doing?
Maria Hi, Sally! I'm writing a schedule.
Sally Why?
Maria Well, I have a lot of work to do, and it's important that I don't forget things. For example, I have a math test next month.
Sally But that's next month! You don't need to think about that now.
Maria I do! It's important to plan now so I don't rush at the last minute.
Sally Are you going to study for two hours every day? That's too much.
Maria Well, I don't know how long I need to study. So it's better to give it two hours in the schedule.
Sally What does it say here? "Relax"? Why are you writing that?
Maria It's important to have time for myself. If I work too hard, I can't focus.
Sally Oh, I see. And why are you coloring it in?
Maria I color the things that are really important red, like my math test, for example. If it's not so important, then it's green.
Sally "Sally's birthday." Ah, thank you, Maria. But hey … why are you coloring that in green?

B **Choose *True* or *False*.**

1 Maria is making a schedule because she has a lot to remember. **True / False**
2 Maria is writing her math test in her schedule at the last minute. **True / False**
3 Maria is sure she needs to study math for two hours every day. **True / False**
4 Maria doesn't want to relax because she wants to focus on her studies. **True / False**
5 Maria colors in things so she doesn't forget them. **True / False**

C **Match the tips about managing your time (1–5) to the reasons (a–e). Write the letter.**

1 Plan time to relax and do something you enjoy. _____
2 Write down due dates in your calendar. _____
3 Decide what is very important and not very important in your to-do list. _____
4 Write down every important task you need to do. _____

a Then you can do the important things first.
b If you feel better, you work better.
c That way you don't forget about it.
d Then you can see how long you have to complete the task.

D IN PAIRS **Role-play. Student A: You are having problems managing your time. Student B: Give Student A advice about managing his or her time.**

Ula: I'm so stressed! I have two exams this week, and I have no time to study!

Tony: Don't worry. Maybe I can help you …

E THINKING SKILL—Predict **What can happen if you don't manage your time well at school or work? Are you good at managing your time? Why or why not?**

MAKE IT HAPPEN

Make a schedule for the next week. Talk with a partner about the ways you can manage your time.

Answers to the quiz on page 116
1 c 2 a 3 c 4 b

UNIT 12 FOLLOW A PRO

A Read about a forest ranger's job. Answer the questions below.

A FOREST RANGER

Forest rangers usually work in national parks and areas of natural beauty. The job can be more dangerous than other jobs, but it's also more enjoyable than an office job for many people. Most rangers in the United States of America work for the Forest Service.

Forest rangers have many jobs. In the summer, when the weather is hotter, they need to prevent fires. They talk about the dangers of forest fires. They tell tourists and schoolchildren about fire safety. They sometimes cut down trees to stop fires. They help firefighters if there's a fire in the forest.

Forest rangers make sure people are safe outdoors. They give information about hiking trails. They teach people how to be safe when camping or hiking in the forest, and how to stay safe from bears and other wild animals. They also help rescue people if they get lost or if things go wrong.

1 Where do forest rangers usually work? __________
2 What do they talk to tourists and children about? __________
3 Why do forest rangers cut down trees? __________
4 What do forest rangers teach people to do? __________

B Discuss the questions as a class.

1 Why is being a forest ranger sometimes a dangerous job?
2 Would you like to work outdoors all the time? Why or why not?
3 What can you do to prevent a fire?

VIDEO

WATCH THE VIDEO AND FOLLOW A BOTANIST.

C IN GROUPS Answer the questions.

1 What is the person's job? __________
2 Where does the person work? __________
3 What skills does the person need for the job? __________
4 Does the person like the job? Why or why not? __________
5 Who does the person work with? __________

D IN GROUPS Check your answers to the quiz on page 126 and discuss the questions.

1 Do you know anyone who works outdoors in nature?
2 What different outdoor jobs do you know?
3 What physical abilities do you need to work outdoors?
4 What are the challenges of working in nature?
5 What skills do you need to work in nature?

Answers to the quiz on page 126
1 c 2 b 3 a 4 a

Irregular Verbs

Infinitive	Simple past	Past participle
be	was/were	been
become	became	become
begin	began	begun
break	broke	broken
bring	brought	brought
build	built	built
buy	bought	bought
catch	caught	caught
choose	chose	chosen
come	came	come
cost	cost	cost
cut	cut	cut
do	did	done
draw	drew	drawn
drink	drank	drunk
drive	drove	driven
eat	ate	eaten
fall	fell	fallen
feed	fed	fed
feel	felt	felt
find	found	found
fly	flew	flown
get	got	gotten
give	gave	given
go	went	gone
grow	grew	grown
hang	hung	hung
have	had	had
hear	heard	heard
hit	hit	hit
hold	held	held
hurt	hurt	hurt
keep	kept	kept
know	knew	known
leave	left	left
let	let	let
lose	lost	lost
make	made	made
meet	met	met
pay	paid	paid
put	put	put
read	read	read
ride	rode	ridden
ring	rang	rung
rise	rose	risen
run	ran	run
say	said	said
see	saw	seen
sell	sold	sold
send	sent	sent
set	set	set
sing	sang	sung
sit	sat	sat
speak	spoke	spoken
stand	stood	stood
stick	stuck	stuck
take	took	taken
teach	taught	taught
tell	told	told
think	thought	thought
throw	threw	thrown
understand	understood	understood
wake	woke	woken
wear	wore	worn
win	won	won
write	wrote	written

Pronunciation Symbols

Vowels

ɪ	did
ɛ	bed
æ	bad
ʌ	cup
ʊ	book
ə	banana
i	feed
ɑ	father, box
ɔ	tall
u	student, food
ɝ	shirt, birthday
eɪ	date, table
aɪ	cry, eye
ɔɪ	boy
oʊ	comb, post
aʊ	about, how

Consonants

p	park, happy
b	back, hobby
t	tea
d	die
k	came, kitchen, quarter
g	game, go
f	face, photographer
V	vegetable
θ	thing, math
ð	then, that
s	city, summer
z	please, goes
ʃ	she, shop
ʒ	leisure
h	hot, who
tʃ	chicken, watch
dʒ	jacket, orange
m	men
n	sun, know
ŋ	sung, singer
w	week, white
r	rain, writer
l	light, long
j	yes, use, music

Grammar Review

A Match the sentence beginning (1–8) to the sentence end (a–h). Write the letter.

1 What's your name? ____
2 Is he your father? ____
3 Where are you from? ____
4 How old is she? ____
5 Are you and Jill from Canada? ____
6 Is her name Maria? ____
7 Who's that? ____
8 Are they Colombian? ____

a I'm from Mexico.
b No, we're not.
c That's Etsuko.
d Yes, he is.
e No, they're not.
f My name's Greg.
g Yes, it is.
h She's 18.

B Look at the picture. Complete the sentences with the words from the box.

a an any are is isn't aren't some

1 There ________ a small bed.
2 There ________ any pens on the desk.
3 There ________ a laptop on the bed.
4 There ________ some keys on the desk.
5 There's ________ bag in front of the desk.
6 There aren't ________ chairs.
7 There's ________ umbrella next to the desk.
8 There are ________ books on the bed.

C Complete the sentences with the correct form of the verb in parentheses.

1 She ________ (work) in a large office in Chicago.
2 They ________ (not work) on weekends.
3 I ________ (take) the number 6 bus to school.
4 We ________ (not live) near the train station.
5 Our school ________ (have) a great cafeteria.
6 He ________ (not go) to work by subway.

D **Write the questions. Add *do* or *does* in the correct place.**

1 you / wear a uniform / ? ______________________
2 where / they / go / after work / ? ______________________
3 your teacher / drive / to school / ? ______________________
4 that bookstore / sell / notebooks / ? ______________________
5 how / I / get to / the bus station / ? ______________________
6 who / she / study with / on weekends / ? ______________________

E **Rewrite the sentences with the words in parentheses.**

1 They are late for class. (often) ______________________
2 I do laundry at night. (sometimes) ______________________
3 My sister cleans the house. (hardly ever) ______________________
4 Mr. Sanchez works on Saturday. (usually) ______________________
5 We are at the office by 9:00. (always) ______________________
6 They go shopping on weekends. (never) ______________________

F **Choose the correct option.**

1 Eric is a good singer, but he **can't to dance** / **cannot dancing** / **can't dance** at all.
2 I **am can speak** / **can speak** / **can speaks** two languages—Spanish and English.
3 Where **do I can get** / **can I get** / **can I to get** some coffee?
4 **Can you play** / **Do you can** / **Can you playing** the piano?
5 She **can't drive** / **can't drive** / **can't drives** a car.
6 What sports **can you play** / **is it can play** / **can't you played** well?

G **Complete the sentences about what is happening right now. Use the words in parentheses.**

1 Kevin ______________ (read) a book.
2 Alex and Jan ______________ (not feel) well.
3 Mark and I ______________ (play) a video game.
4 It ______________ (rain).
5 Those students ______________ (not listen).
6 The teacher ______________ (check) our work.
7 It ______________ (not snow).
8 You ______________ (work) very hard.

H **Choose the correct option.**

Ana: Let's make **1 a** / **some** list before we go shopping.

Will: Good idea. So, what do we need?

Ana: Let's see ... well, we don't have any **2 vegetables** / **vegetable**, so let's get **3 some** / **any** tomatoes and carrots.

Will: OK. And I want to make **4 an** / **some** omelet for breakfast. Do we have **5 an** / **any** eggs?

Ana: Um ... yes, we do.

Will: How **6 many** / **much**?

Ana: Just two, so let's get some. And how about I make cheeseburgers for dinner?

Will: Sounds great! How **7 many** / **much** beef do you want?

Ana: Half a kilo. And don't forget the cheese. We don't have **8 any** / **some**.

Grammar Reference

UNIT 1 — *be* statements and *yes/no* questions

Function

We use *be* to talk about a name, age, job, or where someone or something is or is from. We use *yes/no* questions to ask if something is true or a fact.

Form

Affirmative		Negative	
I am (I'm)	in English 4.	I am not (I'm not)	in English 5.
You are (You're)	an English teacher.	You are not (You aren't)	a Spanish teacher.
He is (He's) She is (She's) It is (It's)	from Colombia.	He is not (He isn't) She is not (She isn't) It is not (It isn't)	from Panama.
We are (We're) They are (They're)	students.	We are not (We aren't) They are not (They aren't)	teachers.

Yes/no questions		Affirmative short answer	Negative short answer
Am I	in English 5?	Yes, you are.	No, you are not. (No, you aren't.)
Are you	a Spanish teacher?	Yes, I am.	No, I am not. (No, I'm not.)
Is he Is she Is it	from Panama?	Yes, he is. Yes, she is. Yes, it is.	No, he is not. (No, he isn't.) No, she is not. (No, she isn't.) No, it is not. (No, it isn't.)
Are we Are they	in Miami?	Yes, we are. Yes, they are.	No, we are not. (No, we aren't.) No, they are not. (No, they aren't.)

A Match the sentence beginning (1–5) to the sentence end (a–e). Write the letter.

1 She ____
2 You ____
3 They're ____
4 I ____
5 It ____

a isn't Mexican food.
b 's a Spanish teacher.
c 'm not from Canada.
d aren't in Class 5.
e from Bahia.

B Complete the sentences.

1 Are we in Class 6? Yes, we __________.
2 Is it from Germany? No, it __________.
3 __________ you from Chile? Yes, I am.
4 Are they American? No, they __________.
5 Is she a yoga teacher? Yes, she __________.
6 __________ your first name James? No, it isn't.

UNIT 1 — information questions with *be*

Function

We use information questions when the answer is a thing (*what?*), person (*who?*), place (*where?*), way (*how?*), or time/date (*when?*).

Form

The word order in information questions with *be* is question word + *be* + word/phrase.

Question	Answer
What is your favorite food?	My favorite food is pizza.
Who is your favorite singer?	My favorite singer is Rihanna.
Where are you from?	I'm from Guatemala.
How are you?	I'm fine.
When is your birthday?	My birthday is May 2.

A Complete the sentences with the correct *wh–* word.

1 ____________ old are you? I'm 17 years old.
2 ____________ is Manuel? He's at home.
3 ____________ is the teacher's last name? It's Sanchez.
4 ____________ is English class? It's at 10:00.
5 ____________ is your favorite actor? It's Leonardo DiCaprio.

B Choose the correct option.

1 What / Where is the teacher?
2 How / What is your email address?
3 What your hobbies are / are your hobbies?
4 Who / When is your favorite musician?
5 When / Where is her birthday?
6 How old they are / are they?

UNIT 2 — articles *a*, *an*, and no article

Function

We use the articles *a* and *an* before a noun or adjective + noun. We do not use *a* or *an* before plural nouns.

Form

Singular nouns	Plural nouns
***a* + consonant sounds (b, c, d, f, g, etc.)**	**no article**
He's a doctor. I have a small family. She studies at a university.	We're students. I have two sisters. Pilots make a lot of money.
***an* + vowel sounds (a, e, i, o, u, etc.)**	
I'm an accountant. She has an interesting job.	

A Choose *a* or *an*.

1 Paulo has a / an great job.
2 Are you a / an interior designer?
3 Sun-hee is a / an new student.
4 My father is a / an engineer.
5 I have a / an older sister.
6 A / An teacher's job is very important.

B Write *a*, *an*, or *X* (no article).

I think I have **1** ______________ interesting job. I work at **2** ______________ water park. I help **3** ______________ people at my ride. It's **4** ______________ very popular ride. Some people ride it many **5** ______________ times. I know **6** ______________ children like the ride.

UNIT 2 — possessive adjectives and *'s/s'*

Function

We use possessive adjectives and *'s/s'* to show possession or how two people are connected. Possessive adjectives and *'s/s'* agree in number with the possessor, not the thing it possesses or is connected to.

Do not confuse possessive *'s* (*Jack's sister is here.* = *His sister is here.*) with the contraction of *is* (*Jack's here.* = *Jack is here.*). Similarly, do not confuse *Whose* to ask about possession (*Whose book is this?*) with the contraction *Who's* (*Who's that?* = *Who is that?*).

Form

Possessive adjectives	
My Your His Her Its Our Their	home is small.

Add *'s* for singular and irregular nouns.
Jennifer's husband is from England. The children's teacher is Mrs. Lynn.
Add *s'* for plural nouns.
My sisters' names are Lucia and Isobel. Our parents' hometown is Los Angeles.

A Complete the sentences with the correct possessive adjective.

1 My neighbor John is from Canada. I think ______________ wife is from France.
2 I see you are from Japan. What's ______________ hometown?
3 That's Mr. and Mrs. Carlson. ______________ first names are James and Alice.
4 That's my sister. ______________ name is Jennifer. She's 16 years old.
5 My sister and I are in the same Spanish class. ______________ teacher is Mr. Cortez.
6 Hello. ______________ name is Chloe. It's nice to meet you.

B Rewrite the sentences. Add *'s* or *s'* to the correct words.

1 Tim and Marta are Susan parents. ______________
2 Max new friend is from India. ______________
3 Our grandparent home is in Florida. ______________
4 Their parent names are Anna and Peter. ______________
5 My brother wife is an interior designer. ______________
6 The children teacher is married. ______________

UNIT 3 — simple present statements and *yes/no* questions

Function

We use the simple present tense to talk about likes and dislikes, preferences, habits, and routines.

Form

Affirmative statements		Negative statements	
I You We They	love soccer.	I You We They	don't like baseball.
He She It	likes to watch soccer. starts at 3:30.	He She It	doesn't like to play soccer. doesn't start at 3:00.

Yes/no questions			Short answers
Do	I you we they	need a ticket?	Yes, I do. / No, I don't. Yes, you do. / No, you don't. Yes, we do. / No, we don't. Yes, they do. / No, they don't.
Does	he she it	have a ticket? start at 3:30?	Yes, he does. / No, he doesn't. Yes, she does. / No, she doesn't. Yes, it does. / No, it doesn't.

A Choose the correct option.

Joe: Hey, Chris. **1** Do you want / Do you wants to watch the soccer game? My brother **2** has / does have a big new TV.

Chris: Umm, no, I **3** doesn't / don't. I **4** don't like / don't likes soccer. Sorry. I **5** prefer / prefers baseball. Is there a game on?

Joe: I think so, but it **6** doesn't start / don't start until 8:00.

Chris: **7** Does your brother / Do your brother like baseball?

Joe: Yes, he **8** does / doesn't. He **9** love / loves all sports.

B Complete the sentences with the correct form of the verb in parentheses.

1 My father and I ______________ (love) to watch sports together.
2 My aunt ______________ (prefer) to listen to modern music.
3 ______________ you ______________ (know) of any cool new sports apps?
4 Richie and Amelia ______________ (not like) to go to concerts.
5 ______________ your friend Mandy ______________ (want) to join our music club?
6 He's a good singer, but he ______________ (not like) to sing alone.

Grammar Reference

UNIT 3 — the imperative

Function

We use the imperative to give orders or instructions. Add *please* to sound more polite.

Form

Affirmative	Negative
Listen to this song. Please buy a ticket for me. Be happy.	Don't sit there. Please don't wait for me. Don't be sad. It's OK.

A Complete the sentences with the correct affirmative or negative form of the verbs in the box.

be buy forget go read turn up

1 __________ to the festival before 9:00 to get good seats.
2 __________ to call me later. I need to talk to you.
3 __________ this book sometime. It's a very interesting story.
4 Please __________ the music. I really want to hear this song.
5 __________ tickets at the stadium. Get them online to save money.
6 I'm sorry about missing your party. Please __________ angry.

UNIT 4 — simple present information questions

Function

We use a *wh–* question word to ask an information question.

Form

Information questions				Answers
Where What When	do	I you they	sit? do on weekends? get up on weekends?	You sit over there. I meet my friends. They get up at 9:00.
Why How Who	does	he she it	like his job? get to school? belong to?	He likes it because it's fun. She takes a bus. It belongs to me.

A Unscramble and write questions.

1 work / do / get to / how / they / ? __________
2 her parents / she / when / does / talk to / ? __________
3 eat lunch / he / where / does / every day / ? __________
4 study with / who / do / they / ? __________
5 does / what / he / do / in his free time / ? __________
6 your / do / like / why / you / job / ? __________

B Look at the answers. Write the questions.

1 Where ______________________________? He works in a bank.
2 Who ______________________________? We live with our parents.
3 When ______________________________? Class starts at 10:00.
4 Why ______________________________? She works there because it's fun.
5 How ______________________________? I feel fine.
6 What ______________________________? They drink coffee every morning.

UNIT 4 — frequency adverbs

Function

We use frequency adverbs to say how often we do something. Note that the adverb goes after the verb *be*, but before other verbs. The adverb *sometimes* can also go at the beginning of a sentence. (*I sometimes drive to work.* = *Sometimes I drive to work.*)

Form

Frequency adverb	Frequency	Example
always	100%	She always takes the subway to school.
usually		I usually get up at 9:00 on weekends.
often		We often eat in the school cafeteria.
sometimes		Do you sometimes listen to podcasts?
hardly ever		They are rarely in the library.
never	0%	Our teacher is never late for class.

A Choose the correct option.

My friend Adam is a real health nut. He **1 is often** / **often is** in the gym. He teaches a fitness class several times a week. He **2 is always** / **always is** early for this class. After his class, he **3 runs usually** / **usually runs** and lifts weights. He watches what he eats. He **4 eats rarely** / **rarely eats** in fast-food restaurants. He **5 has never** / **never has** desserts like ice cream or cake. But he **6 has sometimes** / **sometimes has** chocolate.

B Compete the sentences with the correct frequency adverb from the box.

always never rarely usually

1 Josh ____________ drives to work. He doesn't have a driver's license, so he always takes the bus.
2 Caroline ____________ drinks tea—maybe just once or twice a year.
3 We ____________ eat lunch in the school cafeteria. We eat there from Monday to Saturday.
4 I'm ____________ on time for class. I'm never late, so I have a perfect attendance record.

UNIT 5 — adjectives

Function

We use adjectives to add information to nouns. They can come after *be* (*The people are nice.*). They come before the noun they describe (*nice people*).

Form

After the noun	Before the noun
This café is popular.	This is a popular café.
My hometown is boring.	My hometown is a boring place.
Those houses are expensive.	Those are expensive houses.
They are very interesting.	They are very interesting people.

A Rewrite each sentence to include adjective + noun.

1 That city is dangerous. ____________________
2 Those people are friendly. ____________________
3 This apartment is cheap. ____________________
4 These directions are clear. ____________________

B Read and choose.

There are many interesting neighborhoods in São Paulo, Brazil. Take Vila Madalena, for example. The **1** lively cafés / cafés are lively, and there are excellent shops and art galleries. Make a **2** quick stop / stop quick to look at the many **3** colorful paintings / paintings colorful while you walk down the busy streets. **4** Smart shoppers / Shoppers are smart also visit the traditional markets. Here prices are low and **5** friendly people / people are friendly. Pick up some **6** fresh food / food fresh and chat with the locals.

UNIT 5 — *there is / there are*

Function

We use *there is / there are* to talk about things that exist.

Form

Singular	Plural
Is there a college in this city?	Are there any nice cafés near our school?
Yes, there is. / No, there isn't.	Yes, there are. / No, there aren't.
There's a library.	There are two Mexican restaurants.
There's no train station near here.	There are no good museums in this city.
There isn't a train station near here.	There aren't any good museums in this city.

A Complete the conversation with the words from the box.

Are there Is there There There are There aren't There's

Nina: I really like Lisbon. It's a beautiful city. And the food is excellent.
Rosa: I agree. **1** _____________ some great restaurants and cafés here.
Nina: **2** _____________ any Brazilian restaurants? I love Brazilian food.
Rosa: Oh, yes. **3** _____________ any in this neighborhood. But I know one across the city.
Nina: **4** _____________ a bus we can take there? I'm so hungry!
Rosa: **5** _____________ is no bus stop near here, sorry. **6** _____________ one four or five blocks away.
Nina: Well, let's go!

UNIT 6 — present progressive

Function

We use the present progressive to talk about things that are happening now.

Form

Affirmative statements	Negative statements
I'm texting my brother.	I'm not texting my sister.
You're buying speakers.	You're not / You aren't buying headphones.
He's using his tablet.	He's not / He isn't using his computer.
She's filming with her webcam.	She's not / She isn't filming with her phone.
It's starting now.	It's not / It isn't ending now.
We're feeling surprised.	We're not / We aren't feeling embarrassed.
They're listening to a podcast.	They're not / They aren't listening to music.

Information questions		*Yes/no* questions	
What are you doing?	I'm watching a video.	Are you using your phone?	Yes, I am. / No I'm not.
Who is she texting?	She's texting her cousin.	Is he calling his parents?	Yes, he is. / No, he's not.
Why are they downloading that song?	They're downloading it because they love it.	Are they looking for the file?	Yes, they are. / No, they're not.

A Complete the sentences with the present progressive form of the verb in parentheses.

1 I ______________ (chat) with my grandparents.
2 Max ______________ (not use) his laptop right now.
3 Jill ______________ (text) her friend about the party.
4 Paul ______________ (listen) to his favorite band.
5 Wendy and Steve ______________ (not watch) the movie.
6 David and Sarah ______________ (play) video games.
7 I ______________ (not download) any songs right now.
8 Jonathan and I ______________ (wait) for your call.

B Write the question using the present progressive.

1 where / you / go / ? ______________
2 how / she / feel / ? ______________
3 why / they / smile / ? ______________
4 who / I / speaking to / ? ______________
5 what / he / do / ? ______________
6 why / we / stop / here / ? ______________

UNIT 6 — present progressive vs. simple present

Function

We use the present progressive to talk about things that are happening now or around now. We use the simple present to talk about things that happen regularly.

Form

Things that are happening now or around now	Things that happen regularly
I'm playing a video game right now.	I play video games on the weekend.
She's taking three computer classes these days.	She takes three classes every semester.
What music are you listening to right now?	What music do you like to listen to?

A Complete the sentences with the present progressive or simple present form of the verb in parentheses.

Help! **1** ______________ you ______________ (use) your flash drive? I **2** ______________ (need) one. **3** ______________ City Mall ______________ (sell) them? How much **4** ______________ they ______________ (cost)?

What **5** ______________ you ______________ (do)? My friends **6** ______________ (watch) a movie, but I **7** ______________ (not like) it. It's a romantic comedy. I **8** ______________ (prefer) action movies.

9 ______________ you ______________ (watch) the soccer game on TV? My favorite player **10** ______________ (play) in every match, but he **11** ______________ (not play) now. He **12** ______________ (sit) on the bench.

UNIT 7 — *can/can't* (ability)

Function

We use *can/can't* to talk about ability. We use the same form for all nouns and pronouns (*I can sing. / He can sing.*).

Form

<table>
<tr><th colspan="2">Statements</th><th>Yes/no questions</th><th>Answers</th></tr>
<tr><td rowspan="3">I
You
We
They
He
She</td><td rowspan="3">can ride a bicycle.
can't drive a car.</td><td>Can you sing?
Can she take good pictures?</td><td>Yes, I can. / No, I can't.
Yes, she can. / No, she can't.</td></tr>
<tr><th>Information questions</th><th>Answers</th></tr>
<tr><td>What musical instrument can you play?
How many languages can he speak?
Where can we get Mexican food?</td><td>I can play the piano.
He can speak three languages.
You can get it at Rosa's Café.</td></tr>
</table>

A Choose the correct option.

1 Birds **can** / **can't** fly.
2 Babies **can** / **can't** run.
3 Children **can** / **can't** sing.
4 Fish **can** / **can't** swim.
5 Animals **can** / **can't** talk.
6 Computers **can** / **can't** be helpful.

B Complete the sentences about what the people can (✓) and can't (X) do.

	speak Portuguese	play tennis	drive a car
Mark	X	✓	✓
Beth	✓	✓	X
Todd	X	X	✓

Mark **1** ____________ play tennis and **2** ____________. Todd **3** ____________, but he **4** ____________ speak Portuguese or **5** ____________. Beth **6** ____________ ____________, but she **7** ____________ ____________ and **8** ____________.

UNIT 7 — adverbs of manner

Function

We use adverbs of manner to describe actions. They go after the main verb. Add *–ly* to an adjective to form an adverb (*quick–quickly*). There are some irregular adverbs (*fast–fast, hard–hard, good–well*).

Form

Adjective	Adverb
They are noisy eaters.	They eat noisily.
He is a fast runner.	He runs fast.
She is a good dancer.	She dances well.

A Choose the correct form of the word.

1 She is singing **beautiful / beautifully**.
2 They speak English **good / well**.
3 He's a **slow / slowly** runner.
4 They're **quiet / quietly** neighbors.
5 Please pass the ball **careful / carefully**.
6 I'm learning these new rules **easy / easily**.

B Complete each sentence with the adverb form of the adjective in parentheses.

1 Bend your knees ______________. (slow)
2 They don't swim very ______________. (fast)
3 He sometimes speaks ______________ (angry) to me.
4 She plays the piano ______________. (good)
5 Please put the glass down ______________. (gentle)
6 Don't throw the ball ______________. (hard)

UNIT 8 — countable and uncountable nouns

Function

Countable nouns are things and people we can count. They can be singular (*apple*) or plural (*apples*). Uncountable nouns are people or things we can't count. They don't have a plural form (*milk*). We use *How many ...?* with countable nouns and *How much ...?* with uncountable nouns.

Form

Countable nouns		Uncountable nouns
Singular	**Plural**	
I have a banana. We need an egg.	I have three bananas. We need some eggs.	I want some tea. We need some orange juice.
	How many apples are there?	How much bread is there?

A Write *C* (*countable*) or *U* (*uncountable*) for each noun.

1 vegetables ______
2 beef ______
3 water ______
4 grape ______
5 noodles ______
6 potato ______
7 bread ______
8 sugar ______
9 melon ______
10 rice ______
11 carrot ______
12 flour ______

B Choose the correct option.

1 How **many / much** milk do we have?
2 **Is / Are** there butter in the fridge?
3 Do you have **an / some** orange?
4 You need to add **a / some** salt.
5 There **is / are** some onions in this dish.
6 How **many / much** people are at the party?

UNIT 8 — *this/that/these/those*

Function

We use *this/these* to talk about things near us. We use *that/those* to talk about things not near us. We use *this/that* for singular and uncountable things and *these/those* for plural things.

Form

Singular	Plural
This soup is delicious. That restaurant is a 15-minute drive away.	These melons weigh five kilograms each. Those people across the park can't hear us.

A Look at the pictures. Complete the sentences with *this, that, these,* or *those*.

1 How much are ____________ donuts?

2 Can I please have ____________ basket?

3 Is ____________ black jacket on sale?

4 Are ____________ bananas from Peru?

B Choose the correct option.

1 Is this / that your cup of coffee over there? I think it's getting cold.
2 Look at these / those directions here. I don't understand them.
3 Can you hold this / that box for me? It's really heavy and my arms hurt.
4 Who are these / those people in the other room? Do you know them?

UNIT 9 — verb + infinitive or gerund

Function

Some verbs (e.g., *want*, *need*, and *plan*) are followed by an infinitive (*to* + verb). Some verbs (e.g., *enjoy*) are followed by a gerund (verb + *–ing*). Some verbs (e.g., *like*) are followed by either an infinitive or a gerund, with no change in meaning.

Form

Verb + infinitive	Verb + gerund
I want to travel to Mexico. He would like to take a guided tour. She needs to get a passport. We have to buy some souvenirs. They plan to take a vacation soon.	I enjoy traveling by boat. **Verb + infinitive or gerund** They like to visit new cities. They like visiting new cities.

A Find and correct one error in each sentence.

1 She wants get a hotel near the city center. ______
2 Do you need get a new backpack for your trip? ______
3 I don't enjoy to travel in a large group. ______
4 They plan spending two weeks in Thailand. ______
5 He doesn't like to eating in hotel restaurants. ______
6 Would you like visit Europe or Asia? ______

B Read the travel blog. Complete the sentences with the infinitive or gerund form of the verb in parentheses.

I'm here in Oaxaca, Mexico! This city is great. I am enjoying **1** ______ (walk) around the city very much, but tomorrow I plan **2** ______ (take) a guided tour of the market. I want **3** ______ (try) some local food. I like **4** ______ (meet) the local people, but my Spanish is not very good. I really need **5** ______ (study) the language more. I have **6** ______ (buy) some cool souvenirs for my family, and I would like **7** ______ (get) a good price.

UNIT 9 — *should/could* for advice and possibility

Function

We use *should* to give advice to others and *could* to say what is possible for people to do. Both are followed by the base form of a verb (e.g., *should stay, could visit*).

Form

***should* + verb (advice)**
Everyone needs a passport to go overseas. You should get one right away. It's very cold and snowy there right now. You should pack a warm coat.
***could* + verb (possibility)**
There are lots of places to stay. You could stay in a hotel, at a hostel, or with a local family. All the islands in Hawaii are popular. You could visit Oahu, Maui, Kauai, or the Big Island.

A Match the sentence beginning (1–6) to the sentence end (a–f). Write the letter.

1 Don't take a suitcase on your trip. You should ____
2 I hear you like cold weather. You could ____
3 It's very hot there right now. You should ____
4 I want to follow you on your trip. You should ____
5 You don't drive? You could ____
6 Not many people speak English. You should ____

a post updates every few days.
b plan to stay out of the sun.
c take a taxi or a bus to the airport.
d learn some of the local language.
e visit Iceland, Alaska, or even Siberia!
f bring just a small backpack.

UNIT 10 — simple past (affirmative statements)

Function

We use the simple past to talk about states, events, and actions in the past.

Form

We generally add *–ed* to regular verbs (e.g., *walk–walked, live–lived, stop–stopped*).

Regular verbs	**Add *–ed*.**	**listen–listened**
Verbs ending in *e*	Add *–d*.	love–loved
Verbs ending in vowel + consonant	Double the last consonant and add *–ed*.	hop–hopped
Verbs ending in consonant + *y*	Change *y* to *i* and add *–ed*.	copy–copied

There are many irregular simple past forms (e.g., *speak–spoke, take–took, eat–ate*). See the irregular verbs chart on page 139. Notice spelling patterns on the list of irregular verbs.

Affirmative statements	
I You He She It We They	inspired many people. had an interesting life.

A Write the simple past forms of the verbs.

1 eat ____________
2 learn ____________
3 play ____________
4 speak ____________
5 talk ____________
6 become ____________
7 do ____________
8 have ____________
9 cry ____________
10 shop ____________
11 make ____________
12 go ____________

B Write the simple past forms of the verbs.

Look at this picture of my parents. My father was born in Mexico. He **1** ____________ (come) to the US in 1990. He **2** ____________ (work) in Texas for many years. He **3** ____________ (meet) my mother in 1995. They **4** ____________ (get) married two years later. They **5** ____________ (start) a family and **6** ____________ (have) me in 1999. Later they **7** ____________ (move) to California and **8** ____________ (open) a small restaurant. They **9** ____________ (buy) their first home in 2007.

UNIT 10 — simple past (negative statements and questions)

Form

We use *didn't* (*did not*) + the base form of the verb to form negative simple past statements (*didn't work, didn't go, didn't say*). To ask *yes/no* questions, we use *Did* + subject + the base form of the verb (*Did you live there?*). For short answers, we use *Yes* + subject + *did* or *No* + subject + *didn't* (*Yes, we did. / No, we didn't.*). To ask information questions, we use a *wh–* question word + *did* + subject + the base form of the verb (*Where did they grow up?*).

Negative statements		*Yes/no* questions	
I You He She It We They	didn't work hard. didn't have an easy life.	Did you like the story? Did they tell anyone?	Yes, I did. / No, I didn't. Yes, they did. / No, they didn't.
		Information questions	
		What did you talk about? Where did he grow up? Who did they see?	I talked about you. He grew up in Germany. They saw their grandparents.

A Complete the sentences using the negative simple past form of the verbs.

1 They woke up early. They ____________ late.
2 We felt very cold. We ____________ very hot.
3 She had a big family. She ____________ a small family.
4 It seemed like a good idea. It ____________ like a bad idea.
5 I lived in a noisy neighborhood. I ____________ in a quiet neighborhood.
6 He gave a short speech. He ____________ a long speech.
7 We bought an old house. We ____________ a new house.
8 I read an interesting book. I ____________ a boring book.

B Complete the conversation with short answers or the simple past form of the verbs in parentheses.

Diego: **1** ____________ your family ____________ (come) to visit you last weekend?
José: Yes, they **2** ____________ (do). I **3** ____________ (show) them around the city.
Diego: Where **4** ____________ you ____________ (go)?
José: To the beach. But they **5** ____________ (not enjoy) it much.
Diego: **6** ____________ you ____________ (take) them to eat out?
José: No, I **7** ____________ (not do). They **8** ____________ (want) to cook for me. I **9** ____________ (not mind)!

UNIT 11 — *going to*

Function

We use *going to* to talk about future plans and predictions.

Form

Affirmative statements	*Yes/no* questions and short answers	
I'm going to take a summer class. She thinks she's going to fail her exam.	Are you going to stop by later? Is he going to visit his family?	Yes, I am. / No, I'm not. Yes, he is. / No, he isn't.
Negative statements	**Information questions**	
We're not going to travel this summer. It's not going to be very sunny today.	Where are you going to study? When is she going to see Matt?	In London. This winter.

A Complete the conversations with the correct form of *going to* and the verbs in parentheses.

1 A: What **1** ________ you ________ (do) this weekend?
B: I'm not sure. I think I **2** ________ (clean) the house.

2 A: **3** ________ the weather ________ (be) nice tomorrow?
B: No, it isn't. It **4** ________ (rain) all day.

3 A: Gina **5** ________ (not work) on the project with me.
B: Oh, no! **6** ________ anyone ________ (help) you?

4 A: When **7** ________ your parents ________ (visit)?
B: On Friday. They **8** ________ (spend) the weekend with me.

5 A: **9** ________ you and Rex ________ (get) married?
B: Yes, we are, but we **10** ________ (not have) a big wedding.

UNIT 11 — direct and indirect objects

Function/Form

Some verbs take both an indirect object (often a person) and a direct object (often a thing).

Subject	Verb	Indirect object	Direct object
I He	am going to make sent	her us	a cake. a nice gift.

When the direct object comes first, we need to add the preposition *for* for the verbs *buy, cook,* and *make* and the preposition *to* for the verbs *bring, give, send, sell, show,* and *tell*, before the indirect object.

Subject	Verb	Direct object	Preposition	Indirect object
I He	am going to make sent	a cake a nice gift	for to	her. him.

A Complete the sentences with the words in parentheses. Put the indirect object first.

1 Sorry, but I didn't give ______________. (your message / Maggie)
2 They aren't going to show ______________. (me / their new car)
3 Can you please show ______________? (your new home / us)
4 Gregory is going to buy ______________. (his wife / a surprise gift)
5 We want to make ______________. (a nice dinner / you)
6 Are you going to bring ______________? (your mother / flowers)

B Rewrite the sentences. Put the direct object first.

1 I gave him the letter. ______________
2 I didn't buy her a gift. ______________
3 Let's cook your parents dinner. ______________
4 I want to show you something. ______________
5 She sold me her used car. ______________
6 I'm going to make you some soup. ______________

UNIT 12 — comparative adjectives

Function

We use comparative adjectives to compare two people or things. We use *than* after the adjective (e.g., *The Pacific Ocean is bigger than the Atlantic Ocean.*).

Form

Use	Example
For most one-syllable adjectives, add *–er*.	warm–warmer quick–quicker
For one-syllable adjectives ending in *–e*, add *–r*.	nice–nicer wide–wider
For one-syllable adjectives ending in consonant + vowel + consonant, double the final consonant and add *–er*.	red–redder wet–wetter
For one-syllable adjectives ending in consonant + *y*, and for two-syllable adjectives ending in *y*, change the *y* to *i* and add *–er*.	dry–drier sunny–sunnier
For most other adjectives with two or more syllables, use *more* or *less* + adjective.	more expensive less interesting
Some adjectives have irregular comparative forms.	good–better bad–worse
Some one-syllable adjectives use *more* and *less*.	fun–more fun, less fun

A Write the comparative form for the adjectives.

1 large __________
2 hot __________
3 happy __________
4 bad __________
5 beautiful __________
6 easy __________
7 near __________
8 windy __________
9 big __________
10 important __________
11 thin __________
12 good __________

B Write one sentence that compares two things. Use the adjective in parentheses and add *than*.

1 Mt. Kilimanjaro > Mt. Etna (high)

____

2 the Atacama Desert > the Gobi Desert (dry)

____

3 Iceland > Spain (cool)

____

4 the Amazon River > the Mekong River (wide)

____

5 a plane ticket > a bus ticket (expensive)

____

6 an A+ grade > a C– grade (good)

____

UNIT 12 — review of tenses

Function/Form

Use	Example
We use the simple present to talk about likes, dislikes, preferences, habits, and routines.	I like traveling in a small group. Martin goes camping every summer.
We use the present progressive to talk about things that are happening now.	I'm waiting for the rain to stop. Cindy is updating her blog right now.
We use the simple past to talk about states, events, and single actions in the past.	I went to Costa Rica last year. Hannah hurt her ankle on the hike.
We use *going to* to talk about plans and predictions.	I'm going to visit Iguazu Falls next year. It's going to start snowing soon.

A Complete the paragraph. Use one of the four tenses in the chart and the verb in parentheses.

I **1** __________ (love) to travel. I **2** __________ (go) to a different place every year. Last year, my friend and I **3** __________ (visit) the Grand Canyon, in Arizona. We **4** __________ (fly) to Las Vegas and then **5** __________ (take) a bus from there. We **6** __________ (spend) five days at the canyon. Right now, I **7** __________ (think) about my next trip. I am **8** __________ (go) to Arizona again. I **9** __________ (want) to see Monument Valley. I am **10** __________ (drive) there. Many tourists **11** __________ (visit) this amazing place every year.

Macmillan Education
4 Crinan Street
London N1 9XW
A division of Macmillan Education Limited

Companies and representatives throughout the world

Speak Your Mind Level 1 Student's Book ISBN 978-1-380-01306-4
Speak Your Mind Level 1 Student's Book + access to Student's App and Digital Workbook ISBN 978-1-380-03103-7
Speak Your Mind Level 1 Student's Book + access to Student's App ISBN 978-1-380-03102-0

Written by Mickey Rogers, Joanne Taylore-Knowles and Steve Taylore-Knowles

First published 2020

Designed by QBS Learning
Illustrated by Jerome Brasseur (Beehive Illustration) p. 68 (t), p. 110; Lon Eric Craven (Wendy Lynn & Co.) p. 42; Daniel Deamo (Lemonade Illustration) pp. 21, 81, 90, 153; Keith Favazza (Wendy Lynn & Co.) pp. 70, 75; Bunky Hurter (Mendola Artists) pp. 82, 92; QBS Learning pp. 41, 52, 68(c), 80, 140.
Original cover design by therestless.co.uk
Cover adaptation by Roberto Martinez
Cover photographs by **Getty Images**/PeopleImages (upper body), Getty Images/Tim Robberts (lower body), Getty Images/Chatuporn Sornlampoo/EyeEm (background); **Shutterstock**/REDPIXEL.PL (window).
Picture research by Fernanda Rocha/Ikonia LLC

Authors' acknowledgements
Mickey, Jo and Steve would like to thank everyone at Macmillan Education and RedNova Learning who have made this project possible and who have gone the extra mile (literally!) to meet up, work together, and throw around a million ideas, some of which even made their way into the books! They would also like to thank Scout for her patience and understanding and for letting her parents get on with it when they needed to!

The publishers would like to thank all the teachers that piloted and reviewed the series, and a special thanks to Annette Flavel for content and cultural reviews.

The authors and publishers would like to thank the following for permission to reproduce their photographs:
Alamy Stock Photo/Blend Images p. 50(4), Alamy Stock Photo/Buiten-Beeld p. 118(mr), Alamy Stock Photo/Cliff Hide General News p. 74(r), Alamy Stock Photo/Lev Dolgachov p. 72(1), Alamy Stock Photo/Vadym Drobot p. 101(r), Alamy Stock Photo/Thanapol Kuptanisakorn p. 100(b), Alamy Stock Photo/Robert Preston Photography p. 122(tl), Alamy Stock Photo/Dmitry Rukhlenko – Travel Photos p. 72(8); **Getty Images**/Afonskaya p. 124, Getty Images/AFP/TONY KARUMBA p. 98(br), Getty Images/Robert Alexander p. 120(bl), Getty Images/ullstein bild p. 122(tcr), Getty Images/Blend Images p. 50(5), Getty Images/Blend Images/Mike Kemp p. 72(3), Getty Images/bowdenimages p. 112(3), Getty Images/Brand X Pictures/Hero Images p. 20(Alicia), Getty Images/Paul_Brighton p. 78(cl), Getty Images/Peter Cade p. 30, Getty Images/Caialmage/Dan Dalton, Getty Images/Caialmage/Tom Merton p. 40(t), Getty Images/Caiaimage/Chris Ryan p. 19, Getty Images/Cosmo Condina p. 120(tl), Getty Images/Peter Dazeley p. 82(2), Getty Images/DigitalVision/Hill Street Studios LLC p. 20(Billy), Getty Images/DigitalVision/Lucy Lambriex p. 10(m), Getty Images/Dina Belenko Photography p. 131, Getty Images/elenaleonova p. 42(7), Getty Images/Reza Estakhrian p. 112(1), Getty Images/Eyewire p. 128, Getty Images/E+/AIMSTOCK p. 22(5), Getty Images/E+/AJ_Watt p. 101(l), Getty Images/E+/Yuri_Arcurs p. 20(Tim), Getty Images/E+/asiseeit p. 12, Getty Images/E+/filadendron p. 105(6), Getty Images/E+/fotografixx p. 48(l), Getty Images/E+/franckreporter p. 105(7), Getty Images/E+/GCShutter p. 101(b), Getty Images/E+/Neustockimages p. 114(bl), Getty Images/E+/olaser p. 105(5), Getty Images/E+/shapecharge p. 112(5), Getty Images/E+/xavierarnau pp. 20(Mike), 93(4), Getty Images/E+/Gang Zhou p. 72(4), Getty Images/E+/jcrosemann p. 107(wallpaper), Getty Images/Michele Falzone p. 122(tcl), Getty Images/Pawel Gaul p. 122(br), Getty Images/gdinMika p. 87, Getty Images/Ghislain & Marie David de Lossy p. 114(br), Getty Images/gregobagel p. 74(l), Getty Images/Tom Grill p. 102(1), Getty Images/Craig Hastings pp. 120(ml), 122(bc), Getty Images/Hero Images pp. 20(Ray, Kayla), 22(1,8), Getty Images/Corey Hochachka/Design Pics p. 22(b), Getty Images/Hoxton/Ryan Lees p. 20(Paul), Getty Images/ibreakstock p. 28, Getty Images/Image Source p. 112(6), Getty Images/iStock/artisteer p. 63(A), Getty Images/iStock/cinoby p. 50(br), Getty Images/iStock/Antonio_Diaz p. 60(2b), Getty Images/iStock/DMEPhotography p. 14(bl), Getty Images/iStock/jenifoto p. 55(b), Getty Images/iStock/jeremyiswild p. 102(2), Getty Images/iStock/masta4650 p. 72(2), Getty Images/iStock/Netalieh p. 82(9), Getty Images/iStock/padchas p. 119, Getty Images/iStock/Pinkypills p. 22(3), Getty Images/iStock/RapidEye p. 108, Getty Images/iStock/silverkblack p. 60(4b), Getty Images/iStock/tiler84 p. 32(b), Getty Images/iStock/TommL p. 132, Getty Images/iStock/ViewApart pp. 34, Getty Images/iStock/YinYang p. 20(Cindy), Getty Images/Jacobs Stock Photography Ltd p. 112(4), Getty Images/Jetta Productions Inc. pp. 22(7), 50(8), Getty Images/JGI/Jamie Grill p. 42(8), Getty Images/John & Lisa Merrill p. 32, Getty Images/Johner Images p. 50(2), Getty Images/Jesse Kraft/EyeEm p. 50(bl), Getty Images/Juice Images/altrendo images p. 117, Getty Images/Kirsty Lee/EyeEm p. 60(6), Getty Images/Lonely Planet Images/Michael Marquand p. 120(br), Getty Images/LWA p. 22(4), Getty Images/Jiu Mei Zuo M/EyeEm p. 120(tr), Getty Images/Emilija Manevska p. 60(5), Getty Images/martin-dm p. 60(3b), Getty Images/Maskot p. 55(l), Getty Images/michaeljung p. 35(b), Getty Images/Morsa Images p. 72(7), Getty Images/MuYeeTing p. 122(bl), Getty Images/National Geographic Image Collection Magazines/Jonathan Kingston p. 74(m), Getty Images/Dimitri Otis p. 20(Lynne), Getty Images/Chonlachai Panprommas/EyeEm p. 60(1t), Getty Images/Jose Luis Pelaez Inc. pp. 22(2), 100(t), Getty Images/Jessica Peterson p. 20(Sherry, John), Getty Images/PhotoAlto/Alix Minde p. 60(4t), Getty Images/Edwin Remsberg p. 120(bcl), Getty Images/Science Photo Library p. 60(3t), Getty Images/Selitbul p. 120(tcr), Getty Images/Steve Smith p. 121, Getty Images/SSC p. 42(3), Getty Images/Lisa Stirling p. 82(8), Getty Images/Richard Stonehouse/Stringer p. 98(tr), Getty Images/Tetra Images p. 113, Getty Images/Alex Tihonovs/EyeEm p. 50(6), Getty Images/tororo p. 123, Getty Images/MARIO VAZQUEZ/Stringer p. 122(tr), Getty Images/Klaus Vedfelt p. 112(2), Getty Images/Siwabud Veerapaisarn/EyeEm pp. 46, 130, Getty Images/Bogdan Vija/EyeEm p. 20(Danny), Getty Images/Andreas Vitting p. 120(tcl), Getty Images/Vostok p. 84, Getty Images/Dougal Waters p. 42(5), Getty Images/Westend61 pp. 17, 20(Ellie, Mylie), 23(cl, insets), 27, Getty Images/Michele Westmorland p. 118(tl), Getty Images/Stephen Zeigler p. 20(Eric), Getty Images/10'000 Hours p. 58; Macmillan Publishers/David Tolley p. 82(5); **Shutterstock**/Africa Studio pp. 82(4), 107(man), Shutterstock/andregric p. 62, Shutterstock/antoniodiaz p. 42(2), Shutterstock/Radu Bercan p. 7, Shutterstock/Billion Photos pp. 56, 129, Shutterstock/Wan Faidz p. 78(cr), Shutterstock/Farknot Architect p. 60(2t), Shutterstock/first vector trend p. 127(tr), Shutterstock/fizkes p. 102(3), Shutterstock/flower travelin' man pp. 28, 58, Shutterstock/Art_Photo p. 10(r), Shutterstock/baranq p. 72(cr), Shutterstock/Bobex-73 p. 31, Shutterstock/Orhan Cam pp. 126, 138, Shutterstock/cretolamna p. 28(inset), Shutterstock/DisobeyArt p. 57, Shutterstock/George Dolgikh p. 85, Shutterstock/GK1982 p. 107(boy), Shutterstock/Dean Drobot p. 44, Shutterstock/KucherAV p. 110, Shutterstock/Ekaterina Markelova p. 64, Shutterstock/ESB Professional pp. 6, 55(r), Shutterstock/Rainer Fuhrmann p. 37, Shutterstock/Yuriy Golub p. 72(5), Shutterstock/Barbara Maffei Granadillo p. 78(c), Shutterstock/Grigvovan p. 42(1), Shutterstock/Antonio Guillem p. 24, Shutterstock/haveseen p. 93(2), Shutterstock/Jirsak pp. 66, 135, Shutterstock/Jyliana p. 77, Shutterstock/Lighthunter p. 97, Shutterstock/Lightspring pp. 16, 127(m), Shutterstock/Ocskay Mark p. 8, Shutterstock/GANNA MARTYSHEVA p. 40(b), Shutterstock/mates p. 82(10), Shutterstock/Monkey Business Images pp. 42(4), 50(1,7), 130, Shutterstock/Jaroslav Moravcik p. 94, Shutterstock/Mr Z p. 43, Shutterstock/Tony Northrup p. 120(bcr), Shutterstock/Photographee.eu p. 35(t), Shutterstock/Andrey_Popov p. 22(6), Shutterstock/Pressmaster pp. 86, 136, Shutterstock/Prostock-studio pp. 47, 102(4), Shutterstock/repbone p. 137, Shutterstock/George Rudy p. 67, Shutterstock/Shooting Star Studio p. 99, Shutterstock/sirtravelalot p. 10(l), Shutterstock/Terdsak L p. 128, Shutterstock/Tong_stocker p. 93(1), Shutterstock/Syda Productions pp. 60(7,8), 88, Shutterstock/Awirut Somsanguan p. 78(r), Shutterstock/Suriya99 p. 93(tl), Shutterstock/Vlad Teodor p. 53, Shutterstock/Sergey Tinyakov p. 93(3), Shutterstock/UfaBizPhotoz p. 42(6), Shutterstock/Denis Val p. 114(mr), Shutterstock/Vgstockstudio p. 38, Shutterstock/YAKOBCHUK VIACHESLAV p. 60(1b), Shutterstock/WAYHOME studio p. 104, Shutterstock/Dmytro Zinkevych p. 127(m); **Superstock**/Matt Dutile/Image Source p. 54; **123RF**/ammentorp p. 72(6), 123RF/Mariia Loginova p. 63(B), 123RF/Andriy Popov p. 50(3).

Additional sources:
p. 26 – Bradley Barth, "Malicious bot traffic climbs 9.5 percent in 2017, says report," *SC Magazine*, 2018, Tweak Library, "27 Interesting Facts about Computer Virus," 2018. p. 56 – UNESCO, *UNESCO Science Report*, 2019; Drew DeSilver, "Few Students Likely to Use Print Books for Research," Pew Research Center, 2013; Dan Ackman, "For 53% Reliable Information, Click Here," *Forbes*, 2003. p. 66 – Vincent Wee, "101 Interesting Facts about Digital Marketing," Tech Edt, 2016; "The 25 Best Cities for Marketing Jobs in 2017," Best Marketing Degrees website, 2017. p. 106 – Sandra Choron, Harry Choron, *Wedding Planning: A Nuptial-pedia*, 2010; PaperStyle, "Fun Facts About Birthdays," 2017; Stefania Sainato, "12 Fun Facts About Wedding Planning," *Bridal Guide Magazine*, 2012. p. 126 – Paul Sims, *Daily Mail*, 2012; Mental Floss, "11 Scientific Benefits of Being Outdoors," 2019.

Printed and bound in Brazil

2025
57